INTRODUCTION

The most common technique used to make bead jewelry in Japan is stringing, which generally involves only nylon thread. However, its popularity is now rivaled by that of bead stitching, a type of beadweaving that involves the use of a needle and fine beading thread. This craft has a long history, dating back as far as 1,500 BC, at which time it was already widespread.

In this book we provide instructions that completely demystify the basic beading stitches. Each lesson begins with thorough, step-by-step instructions for a project that will help you master a particular beading stitch while making a piece of jewelry. The additional projects are opportunities for you to hone your newly acquired skills (and make more beautiful jewelry).

Bead stitching is an extremely satisfying craft for many reasons. Working with beads gives us pleasure (and also helps relieve the stress of daily life). And there's nothing like the feeling of accomplishment you experience when you master a stitch or complete a project.

Happy beading!

Kumiko Mizuno Ito

Design: Junko Ando
　　　Kimie Suto
　　　Hiroe Takagi
　　　Yumiko Watanabe

CONTENTS

Read the notes below before you begin a project.

- ■ Purchase a few more beads than the number indicated for a project, just to be on the safe side.

- ■ Follow the instructions for each project in order, referring to the accompanying drawings.

- ■ In the drawings, "FP bead" means fire-polished bead.

- ■ The finished measurements provided in this book are only benchmarks. Try the jewelry on while you are working on it, and make any necessary adjustments by adding or subtracting beads.

- ■ The techniques introduced in this book are in common use, but the same results can be achieved using other techniques.

BASIC STITCHES:
SPIRAL ROPE (1)

Make a bracelet while learning the spiral rope.

We will guide you through the steps involved in creating the spiral rope stitch. At the end of the lesson, you'll be familiar with the technique and have a beautiful bracelet! Along the way we'll show you how to prepare and work with beading thread and how to pass up through beads. In addition to detailed instructions, we'll give you useful tips along the way.

■Finished measurements:

0.8cm W x 18cm L (Spiral rope: 16cm L)

■Supplies

2.4m beading thread

86 3-mm seed beads (cream)

186 2-mm seed beads (gold-lined transparent)

80 4-mm fire-polished beads (rose)

10-mm fire-polished bead (pink)

1 Spiral rope

To weave the spiral rope stitch, you wrap beads (outer beads) around a central line of beads (core beads). The name comes from the shape created by the stitch (a spiral). This is an easy stitch - one that will look totally different when you change the type of beads used. There are so many variations of the spiral rope stitch that it is sometimes referred to as the "magic stitch." This is the perfect stitch for beginning beaders.

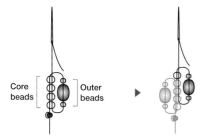

✳ **Spiral rope variations**

Three variations of spiral rope stitch are shown in the photo at left. The core beads in all three are 3-mm seed beads. The outer beads used are gemstone chip beads (left), teardrop glass pearl beads (center), and 2-mm seed beads (right). The nicest thing about this stitch is the transformation spirals undergo when you simply vary the type of beads used.

2 Get your tools and supplies ready.

First gather the tools and supplies you will need. Bead stitching doesn't require bulky or complex equipment, but you will need beading thread and needles in addition to the beads for the bracelet (for details, see pp. 42-43).

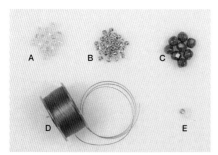

Supplies ✳
A 3-mm seed beads (core beads)
B 2-mm seed beads (outer beads)
C Fire-polished beads (outer beads)
D Beading thread
E Stopper bead

Tools
A Beading needle
B Bead mat
C Measuring tape
D Scissors

✳ You will also need beads for the closure. See p. 4 for details, and for the size and amount of each type of bead

3 Count out the specified number of beads.

Before you start beading, count out the specified number of beads and arrange them in groups on your beading mat. If you don't have a beading mat, use a handkerchief or hand towel. If you place the beads in the order in which they'll be strung, your work will be that much easier (see photo at right).

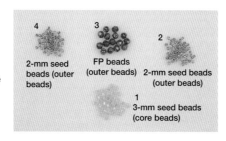

4 2-mm seed beads (outer beads)
3 FP beads (outer beads)
2 2-mm seed beads (outer beads)
1 3-mm seed beads (core beads)

✳ **2-mm (11/0) and 3-mm (8/0) seed beads**

These are the types of beads you'll be using most often. They are cylindrical in shape, although the overall appearance is round. Seed beads are also available in other sizes, including 1.5mm (15/0) and 4mm.

✳ **Fire-polished beads**

The surfaces of these beads are heated for extra roundness and luster. "Fire-polished" is abbreviated as "FP" in our drawings and diagrams.

✳ **Stopper bead**

A stopper bead is strung at the very beginning of a piece to keep the beads you add later from falling off the thread. Remove it after you've finished weaving. A 2-mm (11/0) seed bead is a good choice.

✳ **Bead mats**

When beads are placed on a mat, they're much easier to pass through with the needle, and you don't have to worry about their flying away. Also, it's a good idea to insert the needle into the mat when you're not using it so the thread won't get tangled. Choose a mat that is cushioned and on the thick side.

4　Prepare the thread.

▨ Cutting the thread

It's awkward to work with thread that's too long. Most of the time, you'll want lengths of 1.5-2 meters. For this project, we'll be cutting the thread into 2.4-m lengths so we won't have to add new thread. Hold the scissors so they (re perpendicular to the thread (don't cut on an angle).

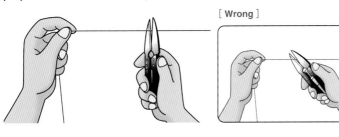

[Wrong]

If you hold the scissors at an angle when you cut, the end of the thread may fray, making it harder to thread the needle.

▨ Smoothing the thread

When you unwind beading thread from a spool, you'll find that it comes off in coils. It would be very difficult to work with that way, so be sure to stretch it once you've cut the length you need.

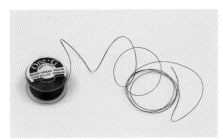
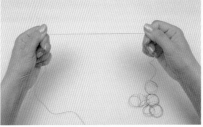

After you've cut the thread, hold a length about as wide as your shoulders and pull on it from both ends; repeat.

＊Cutting the thread

Since nylon thread is coated, the end may disappear into the spool if you cut it right at the edge. We suggest cutting it about 2cm away from the spool.

＊Threading the needle

It's easier to thread the needle against a white background. We recommend doing it over a piece of white paper. If the thread won't slip into the eye easily, drag the end between your teeth to flatten it.

＊Shifting position of needle

In general, position your needle one-third of the way from the thread end (0.5m from the end if you're working with a 1.5-m length of thread). Thread will, of course, get shorter as you weave. Shift position of needle as you work, sliding it along thread, to avoid fraying or breaking of thread.

M a k e　b r a c e l e t .

1　Review the steps you will be following.

Since you won't be replenishing thread this time, you will be weaving from the center out. You'll begin at the center and work toward the right (A). Then you'll work from the center toward the left (B). Once you've learned how to add new thread (see p. 12), you'll be able to weave the band from end to end.

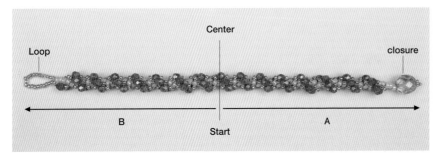

Loop　　　　　　　　　　Center　　　　　　　　　closure

B　　　　Start　　　　A

Once you've threaded the needle, attach a stopper bead (a bead you string on the thread and tie so that the beads don't fall off the thread). A good choice is a 2-mm seed bead in a bright color or a color not used to make the band. Remove the stopper bead when you're finished weaving. For this project, you'll be attaching it at the center of the thread, so move the stopper bead to the correct position before you pass the needle through it again.

❶ String stopper bead on center of thread.

❷ Pass needle through stopper bead again from same direction.

❸ Pull thread to stabilize stopper bead; wind other half of thread around a paper tube.

✳ Stopper bead
The position of the stopper bead will vary according to the piece you are making. To make sure you can remove it easily, make sure you don't sew through the thread inside when you insert the needle into the bead the second time.

✳ Working with a long thread
To keep long thread manageable, wrap it around a piece of paper. Sticky notes are perfect for this purpose. If you attach the thread end to the sticky part, it won't come loose. Use this same method when you have to stop and put your work aside in the middle of a step.

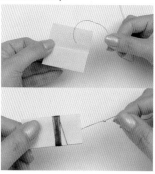

3 **Weave Block A of the spiral rope.**

▨ Stringing beads
The best way to string beads is to pass your needle through them as they lie on the mat. With this method, you can string several beads in succession. If you're using larger beads, put them in your hand and then pass the needle through them.

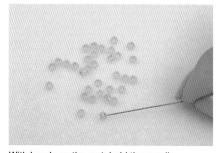

With beads on the mat, hold the needle horizontally and pass it through the beads.

▨ Passing through beads
In bead stitching, you'll be passing the needle through the same beads many times. We often refer to this process as "passing through beads" or "passing the needle through the beads." When you pass through beads, be careful not to sew through other working threads (threads running through the same bead).

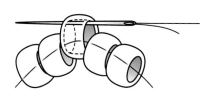

Keep the point of the needle close to the inside wall of the bead to avoid sewing through other beads.

✳ Useful terminology
String (or add) a bead: Pass the needle through a bead for the first time.
Pass through a bead: Pass the needle through a bead that has already been strung.

✳ Beading needles
Designed especially for beadweaving, beading needles are pliant and flexible. They can be inserted into the holes in a series of beads even when the beads are not facing the same way or lying in a straight line.

◼ Begin weaving Block A (Row 1 of outer beads).

Now it's time to begin weaving the spiral rope that forms the band. To make the spiral rope stitch, you first string the 3-mm core beads. Then you add the outer beads so that they line up next to the core beads. Each set of outer beads counts as one row.

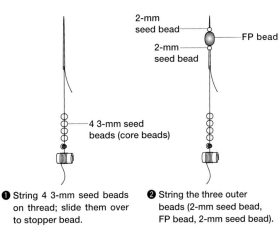

2-mm seed bead
FP bead
2-mm seed bead

4 3-mm seed beads (core beads)

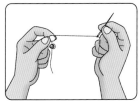

❶ String 4 3-mm seed beads on thread; slide them over to stopper bead.

❷ String the three outer beads (2-mm seed bead, FP bead, 2-mm seed bead).

❸ With outer beads still on needle, pass up through all 4 core beads.

❹ Pull thread gently until outer beads line up next to core beads.

❺ Move outer beads in front of and to left of core beads.

◼ Outer beads (Row 2 and beyond)

In Row 2 and beyond, you will be weaving the same way as in Row 1, except that you'll be adding one 3-mm seed bead (core bead) per row.

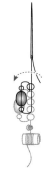

❶ Add one core bead; slide it down on top of 4th core bead.

❷ String 3 outer beads on needle; pass through top 4 core beads from underneath.

❸ Pull thread; move outer beads in front of and to left of core beads.

✳ Pulling thread

Hold the beads in your left hand, and pull with your right. If you hold only the thread when you slide the beads, it may weaken. Your work will go faster if you hold the needle in one hand, and the thread between the thumb and index finger of the other hand; then pull on the thread, a little at a time.

[Wrong]

Don't let the thread rub against the walls or corners of beads, because it will weaken.

✳ Moving the outer beads

It doesn't matter whether you move the outer beads to the left or the right. Just remember to always move them in the same direction.

✳ Thread tension

You will have your own preferences about thread tension. If it's tight, your woven piece will be firm; if you keep it loose, it will be supple. Don't keep it so loose that the beads are sliding around, or so tight that you have trouble passing through core beads.

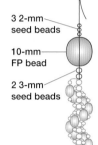

4 Weave spiral rope, repeating Steps ①–③ until you have only 30cm thread left.

5 This is how Block A should look when it's finished; after 40 rows, it should be 8-8.5cm long.

---

4 | **Attach closure to bracelet; finish off thread.**

■ **Attach closure to bracelet.**

Now you will be making a closure at the end of the spiral rope (Block A). You will need at least 30cm thread, so make sure you have enough.

3 2-mm seed beads

10-mm FP bead

2 3-mm seed beads

1 String beads for closure (2 3-mm seed beads, 10-mm FP bead, 3 2-mm seed beads) on thread at end of spiral rope.

2 Pass through FP bead and 2 3-mm seed beads, referring to drawing; pass through 4 core beads.

3 Pass through last set of outer beads; pass through beads in closure, referring to drawing, for added strength.

■ **Finishing off thread**

After making and attaching the closure, run needle back through spiral rope, passing through core and outer beads and making half-hitch knots as you go along.

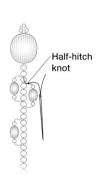
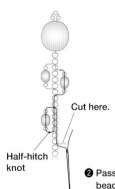

Half-hitch knot

1 Pass up through last core bead strung; bring needle out and make half-hitch knot where indicated in drawing.

Cut here.

Half-hitch knot

2 Pass needle through outer beads and core beads; tie another half-hitch knot and cut thread at edge of a bead.

[Half-hitch knot]

Slide needle under a working thread, wrap thread on needle once around needle, then pull needle through (this is the same knot you make in hand sewing).

✳ **How to hold your beadwork**
Hold beadwork upright so that newly added core beads won't slide off. Drape thread over your index finger and hold it with your middle finger to maintain tension.

✳ **Basic movements**
Hold outer beads on needle with your fingers so they won't slip off. Always slide the outer beads on woven piece in the same direction, holding them down with your thumb.

✳ **Half-hitch knot**
The trick to making this knot is to wrap the thread around needle from front to back.

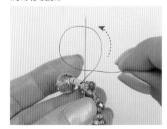

5 · Weave Block B of the spiral rope and make closure loop.

■ Block B

Begin Block B when you have completed Block A. You will be following the same steps, but this time, check the length every now and then.

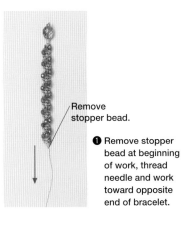

Remove
stopper bead.

❶ Remove stopper bead at beginning of work, thread needle and work toward opposite end of bracelet.

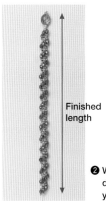

Finished length

[Adjusting the length]

Adjust the length of the bracelet by shortening or lengthening the spiral rope. The length of the bracelet is measured from the closure at the end of Block A to the end of Block B (before you make the loop). Try the bracelet on before you add the loop.

❷ Weave spiral rope of desired length, as you did with Block A.

■ Make loop half of closure.

Now all you need to do is make the loop half of the closure at the end of Block B. For the loop, you will need enough beads to accommodate the bead at other end.

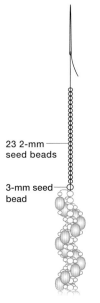

23 2-mm seed beads

3-mm seed bead

❶ String a 3-mm seed bead on thread at end of Block B. Add 23 2-mm seed beads for loop.

❷ Pass through a 3-mm seed bead, a core bead and an outer bead; pass needle through beads in loop once again.

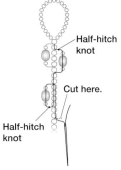

Half-hitch knot

Cut here.

Half-hitch knot

❸ Pass needle through outer beads and core beads, making 2 half-hitch knots as you go along; cut excess thread at edge of a bead.

✻ Direction of work
With the spiral rope stitch, changing the way you hold the woven piece won't affect its appearance.

✻ Removing the stopper bead
You should be able to remove the stopper bead by pulling (gently) on the thread. If you encounter difficulty, use your needle to loosen the thread.

✻ Cutting thread at the edge of a bead
Pull the thread before you cut it at the edge of a bead so you won't have an end sticking out. Patchwork scissors, with their curved blades, make this task easy.

BASIC STITCHES:
SPIRAL ROPE (2)

Make a necklace while learning the spiral rope.

Now we will show you how to make a necklace to match the bracelet shown on p. 4. You can wear these two pieces as a set, or you can join them, as shown in photo below, to make a longer necklace! The necklace is made in exactly the same way as the bracelet, except that you will be learning how to join new thread. You will also be getting accustomed to working with a longer piece.

■Finished measurements:

0.8cm W x 40cm L
(Spiral rope: 38cm)

■Supplies

5.4m beading thread
196 3-mm (8/0) seed beads (cream)
406 2-mm (11/0) seed beads (gold-lined translucent)
190 4-mm fire-polished beads (rose)
10-mm fire-polished bead (pink)

1 Review the steps you'll be following.

The bracelet on p. 4 is woven from the center out. For the necklace, though, you will be learning how to join new thread, so you'll weave from one end to the other.

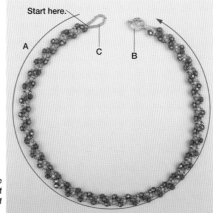

Start here.

A   C   B

First, weave the necklace (A), then add bead half of closure (B) and loop half of closure (C)

2 Weave necklace in spiral rope.

Cut a 5.4-m length of thread, then cut it into 1.8-m lengths. Position the stopper bead 30cm from the thread end (not at the center of the thread, as you did last time). Work the spiral rope stitch the same way you did to make the bracelet.

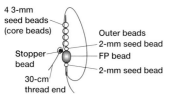

4 3-mm seed beads (core beads)

Stopper bead

Outer beads
2-mm seed bead
FP bead
2-mm seed bead

30-cm thread end

❶ Attach a stopper bead 30cm from thread end and string 4 core beads; with outer beads still on needle, pass through core beads.

❷ Move outer beads to left and string a core bead; with outer beads still on needle, pass through top 4 core beads from underneath.

❸ Repeat Step ② until you have a spiral rope of approximately 190 rows. Use same thread (30cm) for closure.

▓ Joining new thread

When you're working on a long piece like a necklace, join new thread when there is only 20cm thread remaining. For this necklace, you'll be joining new thread twice.

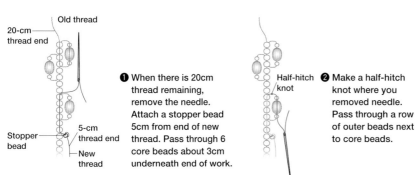

Old thread

20-cm thread end

Stopper bead

5-cm thread end

New thread

❶ When there is 20cm thread remaining, remove the needle. Attach a stopper bead 5cm from end of new thread. Pass through 6 core beads about 3cm underneath end of work.

Half-hitch knot

❷ Make a half-hitch knot where you removed needle. Pass through a row of outer beads next to core beads.

* **How to untangle thread**
If your thread gets tangled, hold woven piece up in the air and let it spin until it untangles.

* **If a knot forms in the thread**
Use the point of a blunt needle (not a beading needle) to poke a hole in the knot. With another blunt needle, widen the hole until you can untie the knot. Do this with care, using a magnifier mirror to avoid damaging the thread.

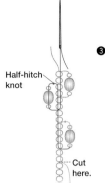

❸ Pass through core beads and tie another half-hitch knot. After you've picked up one row of outer beads and the remaining core beads, you'll reach the end of the piece. Remove stopper bead and cut thread.

Half-hitch knot

Cut here.

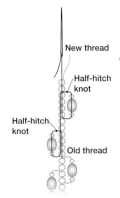

New thread

Half-hitch knot

Half-hitch knot

Old thread

❹ After you've used 3cm new thread, finish off old thread. Pass through core and outer beads woven with new thread, making half-hitch knots as you go; finish off thread.

＊**What if I string the wrong beads?**
The safest thing to do is remove the needle so you won't damage the thread, and pull beads off thread. If you use the needle to remove them, do it with the eye end.

---

3 Attach closure to each end of necklace.

▦ Attach bead for closure

Once necklace is desired length, attach bead half of closure. You will need 30cm of thread, so add new thread now if you have less than that.

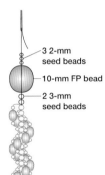

3 2-mm seed beads

10-mm FP bead

2 3-mm seed beads

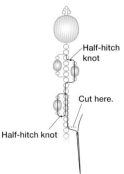

Half-hitch knot

Cut here.

Half-hitch knot

❶ String 2 3-mm seed beads, 10-mm fire-polished bead and 3 3-mm seed beads for closure on thread at end of work.

❷ Pass back through the closure beads; pass up through core beads and outer beads, then closure beads once again.

❸ Pass up through core and outer beads, making 2-3 half-hitch knots as you go along. Cut excess thread at edge of a bead.

＊**Color variation**
The necklace shown in the photo below was made with the same stitch and the same beads, but in different colors. The red fire-polished beads really make this necklace sparkle.

▦ Loop half of closure

Remove stopper bead, thread needle and string beads to form a loop. Attach loop and finish off thread.

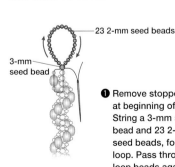

23 2-mm seed beads

3-mm seed bead

❶ Remove stopper bead at beginning of work. String a 3-mm seed bead and 23 2-mm seed beads, forming a loop. Pass through loop beads again, referring to drawing.

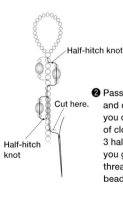

Half-hitch knot

Cut here.

Half-hitch knot

❷ Pass through core and outer beads, as you did for bead half of closure, making 2-3 half-hitch knots as you go. Cut excess thread at edge of a bead.

Lariat

To make this delicate, slender lariat, you add two core beads per row. You'll be amazed at how quickly the work goes. Larger crystal beads attached to the ends of the spiral make lovely accents.

Spike Necklace

This gorgeous spiral rope necklace is reminiscent of the first fruits of summer. Glass-pearl and freshwater-pearl bead spikes, added after the necklace is woven, lend excitement and heft.

Lariat

■Finished measurements:

0.8cm W x 89cm L (Spiral rope: 80cm)

■Supplies

4m beading thread

396 3-mm (8/0) seed beads (silver)

592 2-mm (11/0) seed beads (light green)

99 3-mm glass pearl beads (silver)

49 5-mm glass pearl beads (silver)

49 4-mm bicone crystal beads (blue)

2 12×18-mm bicone beads (gray)

❶ Divide thread into two 2-mm lengths. String a stopper bead on thread, leaving a 50-cm end. Add 4 3-mm seed beads (core beads), then outer beads (A in drawings). Pass through 4 core beads from underneath. Move outer beads to left in front of core beads (Fig. 1).

❷ Row 2: string 2 core beads and outer beads (B in drawings). Pass through top 4 core beads (Fig. 2).

❸ Row 3: string 2 core beads and C outer beads. Row 4: string 2 core beads and D outer beads (Figs. 3 and 4).

❹ Continue weaving, adding 2 core beads on each row. You will be adding A-D outer beads 49 times, then weave one more repetition with A beads. Add new thread when only 20cm thread remains on needle (Fig. 5).

❺ Decorate ends of spiral rope: string beads on thread at end of work; pass needle through decorative beads, referring to drawing, and then back into spiral rope (Fig. 6).

❻ Pass through core and outer beads in spiral rope, making half-hitch knots as you go. Finish off thread.

❼ Remove stopper bead from thread at beginning of work. Add decorative beads, following directions in Step ⑤. Pass needle back into beads in spiral rope and finish off thread.

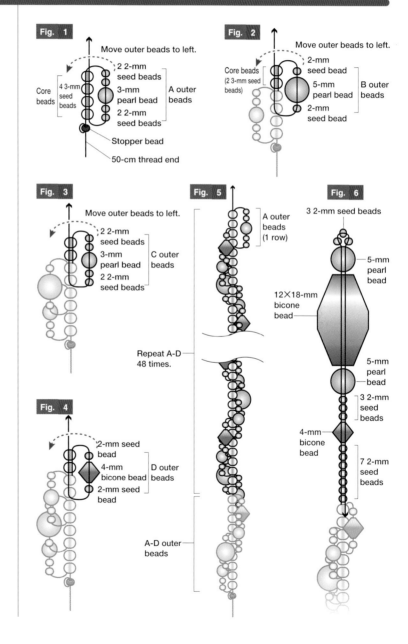

Spike Necklace

■Finished measurements:

0.5-1cm W x 40.5cm L (Spiral rope: 38cm)

■Supplies

[Necklace]
8.8m beading thread
195 3-mm (8/0) seed beads (cream)
590 2-mm (11/0) seed beads (light yellow-green) (A)
190 3.4-mm drop beads (yellow-green)

[Spikes]
672 2-mm (11/0) seed beads (gold-lined translucent) (B)
28 4-mm bicone crystal beads (pale blue)
28 3.5-mm freshwater-pearl rice beads (cream)
28 3-mm glass pearl beads (brown) (A)
28 3-mm glass pearl beads (green) (B)
28 3-mm glass pearl beads (yellow) (C)
Bar-and-ring toggle closure (antique gold)

❶ Divide thread into 1.6-mm lengths. String a stopper bead on thread, leaving a 30-cm end. Add 4 3-mm seed beads (core beads), then outer beads, referring to drawing. Pass through all 4 core beads. Move outer beads to left in front of core beads (Fig. 1).

❷ String a core bead and outer beads, referring to drawing. Pass through top 4 core beads (Fig. 2).

❸ Weave 190 rows of spiral rope stitch, adding one core bead each row.

❹ Attach closure: string a 3-mm seed bead, 4 2-mm seed beads (A), ring of closure and 4 more 2-mm seed beads on thread at end of work, forming a loop. Pass through beads in spiral rope, then beads in loop. Pass needle back into spiral rope and finish off thread, passing through core and outer beads, and making half-hitch knots as you go along.

❺ Remove stopper bead at beginning of work. String a 3-mm seed bead, 6 2-mm seed beads (A), bar of closure, and 6 more 2-mm seed beads, forming a loop. Pass through beads in loop again, referring to drawing, and finish off thread as in Step ④.

❻ Attach spikes to spiral rope: cut thread into 2-mm lengths. Attach a stopper bead, leaving a 20-cm thread end. Pass through core beads on 68th and 69th spirals, and attach a set of glass-pearl bead spikes to 69th spiral, referring to drawing (Fig. 5).

❼ Attach a set of freshwater-pearl bead spikes under core beads in 69th spiral. Pass through 3 core beads (Fig. 6).

❽ Passing through 3 core beads at a time, make 28 sets of spikes, alternating between glass pearl and freshwater-pearl beads. Pass through 2 core beads, pass needle through beads in spiral ropes and finish off thread. Remove stopper bead at beginning of work and finish off thread as in Step ④ (Fig. 7).

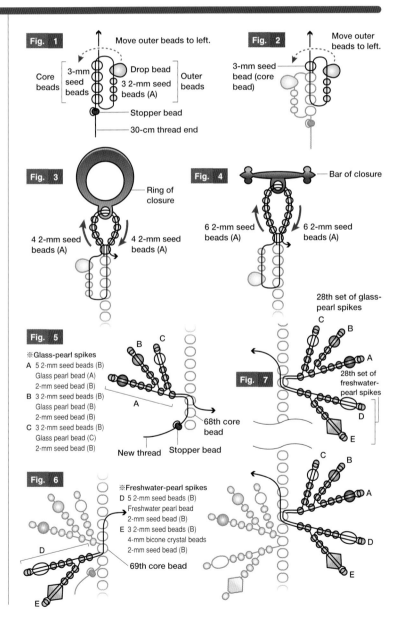

Fig. 1 Move outer beads to left.
Core beads · 3-mm seed beads · Drop bead · 3 2-mm seed beads (A) · Outer beads · Stopper bead · 30-cm thread end

Fig. 2 Move outer beads to left.
3-mm seed bead (core bead)

Fig. 3 Ring of closure
4 2-mm seed beads (A) · 4 2-mm seed beads (A)

Fig. 4 Bar of closure
6 2-mm seed beads (A) · 6 2-mm seed beads (A)

Fig. 5
※Glass-pearl spikes
A 5 2-mm seed beads (B)
 Glass pearl bead (A)
 2-mm seed bead (B)
B 3 2-mm seed beads (B)
 Glass pearl bead (B)
 2-mm seed bead (B)
C 3 2-mm seed beads (B)
 Glass pearl bead (C)
 2-mm seed bead (B)
New thread · Stopper bead · 68th core bead

Fig. 6
※Freshwater-pearl spikes
D 5 2-mm seed beads (B)
 Freshwater pearl bead
 2-mm seed bead (B)
E 3 2-mm seed beads (B)
 4-mm bicone crystal beads
 2-mm seed bead (B)
69th core bead

Fig. 7
28th set of glass-pearl spikes
28th set of freshwater-pearl spikes

Peyote Stitch

Daisy Chain

Herringbone Stitch

MAKE JEWELRY WHILE LEARNING SIX BASIC STITCHES

Now that you've learned some basic weaving techniques and the spiral rope stitch, why not try your hand at some other basic stitches? All six of the stitches introduced here have been in use for centuries, during which regional and national variations have been born. In this section, we begin with the simpler stitches, but feel free to skip to a more challenging stitch if you fall in love with an item of jewelry that features it. The first project in each lesson, with its detailed instructions, is a perfect place to start.

Netting

Brick Stitch

Right Angle Weave

PEYOTE STITCH

Peyote stitch is easily recognizable because it looks like a wall of tiny bricks. It is one of the most popular stitch among beaders, and perhaps the stitch most widely used. The fact that its steps are easy to learn, that it is adaptable to almost every type of design, whether flat or more dimensional, because it's easy to make increases and decreases, and has a wide range of uses.

BASIC

Pearl Cluster Ring

To make this ring, you weave a long, narrow strip of peyote stitch and join the ends to form the band. The pink ring is eight stitches wide, while the bronze ring, with six stitches, is slightly narrower. You can, of course, adjust the width to your liking. We used beads left over from another project to make the freshwater-pearl bead cluster, which gives the ring a glamorous presence.

Royal Ring

Like the basic ring on p. 18, this ring is woven in eight-stitch rows. The combination of brightly colored and translucent beads suggests a decorative border on a royal robe. For the top of the ring, we substituted fire-polished and triangle beads. The number of stitches remains the same, but the larger beads give the ring added volume and effect.

Pearl Cluster Ring

■**Finished measurements:**

Pink ring: 1.2cm W x 6cm L

Bronze ring: 0.9cm W x 6cm L

■**Supplies**

2m beading thread

[Pink ring]

236 2-mm (11/0) seed beads (lavender)

12 1.5-mm (15/0) seed beads (silver-lined pink)

12 5×7-mm freshwater pearl beads (6 white, 6 pink)

[Bronze ring]

180 2-mm (11/0) seed beads (bronze)

12 1.5-mm (15/0) seed beads (silver-lined pink)

12 5×7-mm freshwater pearl beads (6 white, 6 brown)

1 Weave band in peyote stitch.

❶ Rows 1 and 2: make an 8-stitch-wide band. String a stopper bead on thread, leaving a 20-cm end. Add 8 2-mm seed beads (6 for the narrower bronze ring) (Fig. 1).

❷ With a new 2-mm seed bead on needle, pick up 2nd bead from right (Figs. 2 and 3).

❸ Add a 2-mm seed bead. Skip one bead on previous row and pick up 2nd bead (Fig. 4).

❹ Repeat Step ③ twice. You should now have 3 8-stitch rows (Fig. 5).

❺ Starting with Row 4, string one bead and pick up high bead from the previous row; repeat (Fig. 6).

❻ Repeat Step ⑤ until band is long enough to fit around your finger. End on the edge without the stopper bead (Fig. 7).

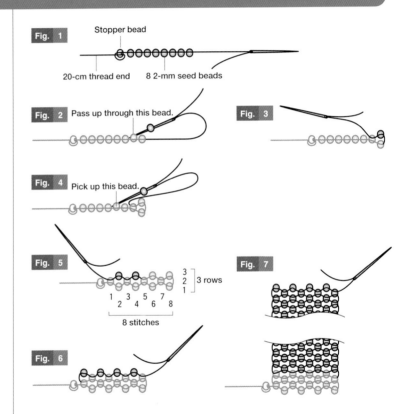

2 Join edges of band and attach pearl cluster.

❶ Using same thread, join edges of band, passing through beads protruding from each one in alternation (Fig. 8).

❷ Pick up first bead strung and run needle through beads in band on the diagonal. Then turn and form an intersection in a bead, referring to drawing. You have just anchored the thread to secure it. Since you will not be attaching the cluster near your thread anchor, go back through

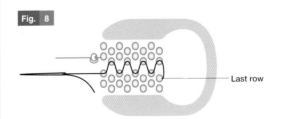

Last row

beads, again on the diagonal, and bring needle out at center of band. Use same thread to attach cluster (Figs. 9 and 10).

❸ String a 2-mm seed bead, a freshwater pearl bead, and a 1.5-mm seed bead on thread. Pick up freshwater pearl bead, 2-mm seed bead, and another 2-mm seed bead from band. Attach 11 more freshwater pearl beads in the same way.

❹ Finish off thread: using same thread, run needle through beads in band, turning to form anchor as in Step ②. Cut excess thread at edge of a bead.

❺ Remove stopper bead at beginning of work. Run needle through beads in band, forming intersections 2-3 times, moving toward end of work. Cut excess thread at edge of a bead.

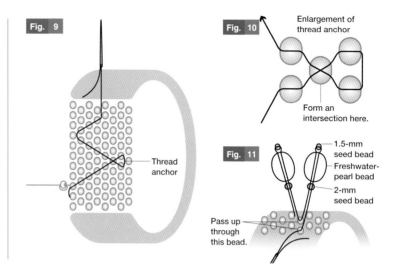

Fig. 9

Thread anchor

Fig. 10

Enlargement of thread anchor

Form an intersection here.

Fig. 11

1.5-mm seed bead
Freshwater-pearl bead
2-mm seed bead

Pass up through this bead.

Instructions

Royal Ring

■**Finished measurements:**

1cm W x 6cm L

■**Supplies**

1.5m beading thread
74 1.6-mm cylinder beads in Color A (white)
74 1.6-mm cylinder beads in Color B (light brown)
58 1.6-mm cylinder beads in Color C (moss green)
58 1.6-mm cylinder beads in Color D (beige)
14 3-mm fire-polished beads in Color A (topaz)
14 3-mm fire-polished beads in Color B (gold-lined translucent)
14 2.5-mm triangle beads (yellow)
Note: Colors in parentheses are for yellow ring.

❶ String a stopper bead on thread, leaving a 20-cm end. String cylinder beads, referring to drawing for color placement (Fig. 1).

❷ Weave 10 rows in peyote stitch, referring to drawing (Fig. 2).

❸ In Rows 11-24, substitute triangle beads for cylinder beads in Color B, fire-polished beads in Color B for cylinder beads in color C, and fire-polished beads in Color A for cylinder beads in Color D. Continue weaving with cylinder beads in Color A (Fig. 3).

❹ Starting with Row 25, substitute cylinder beads for triangle and fire-polished beads. Continue weaving until desired length is reached, ending at edge opposite stopper bead (Fig. 4).

❺ Join ends of band, passing through beads protruding from each one in alternation, with same thread (Fig. 5).

❻ Finish off threads at beginning and end of work.

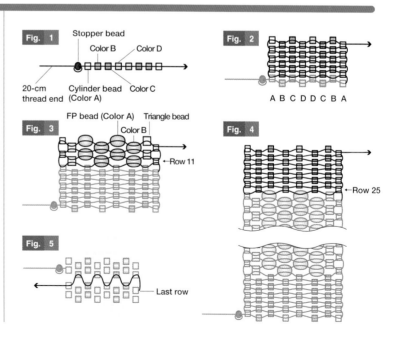

Fig. 1
Stopper bead
Color B   Color D
20-cm thread end   Cylinder bead (Color A)   Color C

Fig. 2
A B C D D C B A

Fig. 3
FP bead (Color A)   Triangle bead
Color B
←Row 11

Fig. 4
←Row 25

Fig. 5
←Last row

DAISY CHAIN

The appealing daisy chain stitch is a series of bead circles (petals) enclosing a central bead. Lines of beads separate the "daisies." This stitch has many variations.

BASIC

Eyeglass chain

This lovely eyeglass chain has lines of silver beads separating turquoise daisies. Silver and turquoise always add up to a winning color combination. Two different sizes of the turquoise beads are used to make small and large daisies. You could also wear this piece as a necklace; just join the two lobster closures!

Bracelet

This colorful piece features two types of daisy chain stitches. The same beads are used for the centers of the daisies, but the petals are formed from two different types and sizes of beads. We've found that it's a good idea to use one type of beads for the petals, and intersperse the "daisies" with other beads that will add color and impact.

Instructions

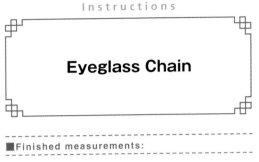

Eyeglass Chain

■Finished measurements:

0.2-1cm W x 83cm L (Daisy chain: 83cm L)

■Supplies

2m beading thread

280 2-mm (11/0) seed beads (silver)

140 2-mm (11/0) seed beads (turquoise)

102 1.5-mm (15/0) seed beads (gold)

56 3-mm round beads (turquoise)

14 3-mm glass pearl beads (white)

7 5-mm glass pearl beads (white)

6 3 x 5-mm button fire-polished beads (turquoise)

2 4×6-mm oval Czech glass beads (turquoise)

14 4-mm metal flower beads (silver)

2 6-mm metal flower beads (silver)

2 lobster closures (silver)

2 eyeglass holders (silver)

1 Weave eyeglass chain in daisy chain.

❶ String a stopper bead on thread, leaving a 20-cm end. Add a 1.5-mm seed bead, 10 silver 2-mm seed beads, and another 1.5-mm seed bead (Fig. 1).

❷ String 10 2-mm turquoise seed beads for daisy (Fig. 2).

❸ Make a small daisy: pick up first turquoise 2-mm seed bead strung, working in same direction, and add a 3-mm pearl bead for center of daisy. Pick up 6th 2-mm seed bead, working in opposite direction (Fig. 3).

❹ String a 1.5-mm seed bead, 5 silver 2-mm seed beads and a 4-mm metal bead, referring to drawing. Add 8 3-mm round beads and a 5-mm pearl bead to make large daisy (Fig. 4).

❺ Repeat the pattern shown in drawing six more times. Omit button bead from end of 7th pattern (Fig. 5).

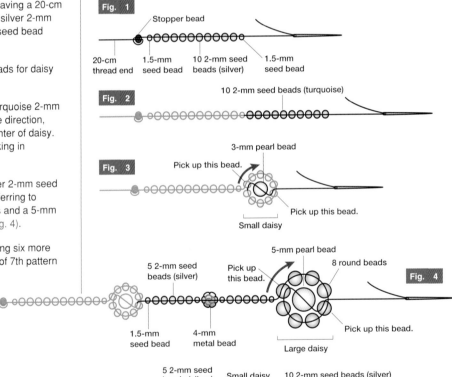

Fig. 1

Stopper bead

20-cm thread end · 1.5-mm seed bead · 10 2-mm seed beads (silver) · 1.5-mm seed bead

Fig. 2

10 2-mm seed beads (turquoise)

Fig. 3

3-mm pearl bead

Pick up this bead.

Pick up this bead.

Small daisy

Fig. 4

5 2-mm seed beads (silver)

Pick up this bead.

5-mm pearl bead

8 round beads

1.5-mm seed bead

4-mm metal bead

Large daisy

Pick up this bead.

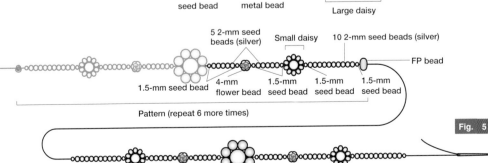

5 2-mm seed beads (silver)

Small daisy

10 2-mm seed beads (silver)

FP bead

1.5-mm seed bead

4-mm flower bead

1.5-mm seed bead

1.5-mm seed bead

1.5-mm seed bead

Pattern (repeat 6 more times)

Fig. 5

7th pattern

❶ String an oval Czech bead, a 1.5-mm seed bead, a 6-mm flower bead, 4 1.5-mm seed beads, lobster closure and 3 more 1.5-mm seed beads on thread. Pass through 1.5-mm seed beads and lobster closure, referring to drawing, to make a loop. Pass needle back through eyeglass chain, making 2 half-hitch knots as you go along. Finish off thread (Fig. 6).

❷ Remove stopper bead at beginning of work. String beads and lobster closure as in Step ①. Finish off thread.

❸ Attach an eyeglass holder to each lobster closure (Fig. 7).

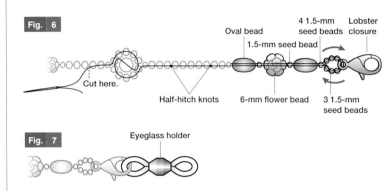

Fig. 6

Oval bead
1.5-mm seed bead
4 1.5-mm seed beads
Lobster closure
Cut here.
Half-hitch knots
6-mm flower bead
3 1.5-mm seed beads

Fig. 7
Eyeglass holder

Instructions

Bracelet

Finished measurements:

1cm W x 18cm L (Daisy chain: 16cm L)

Supplies

1.5m beading thread

16 3-mm round beads (bronze)

12 4-mm round beads (orange)

100 2-mm (11/0) seed beads (gold)

32 3-mm (8/0) seed beads (yellow-green)

3 8-mm round designer beads (turquoise)

3 8×12-mm pressed-glass beads (pale green)

---

❶ String a stopper bead on thread, leaving a 40-cm end. Add beads, referring to drawing. Weave small daisies with 10 3-mm seed beads and a 4-mm round bead, and large ones with 8 3-mm seed beads and a 4-mm round bead (Fig. 1).

❷ Weave bracelet sections in this order: A, B, A, B, A (Fig. 1).

❸ String beads to make closure, referring to drawing. For added strength, pass through beads in a daisy, then pass needle through beads in closure once again. Pass needle back through beads in bracelet and finish off thread, making 2 half-hitch knots as you go (Fig. 2).

❹ Remove stopper bead at beginning of work and string 23 2-mm seed beads (★ in drawing) on thread. Pass through first bead strung to form a loop. Pass through beads in daisy and pass needle through beads in loop again, referring to drawing. Pass needle back through beads in bracelet and finish off thread. Make sure loop accommodates bead half of closure; make adjustments, if necessary (Fig. 3).

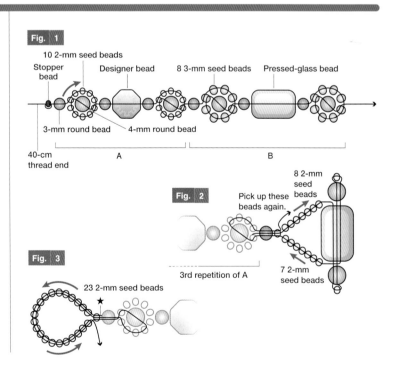

Fig. 1

10 2-mm seed beads
Stopper bead
Designer bead
8 3-mm seed beads
Pressed-glass bead
3-mm round bead
4-mm round bead
40-cm thread end
A
B

Fig. 2
Pick up these beads again.
8 2-mm seed beads
3rd repetition of A
7 2-mm seed beads

Fig. 3
23 2-mm seed beads
★

25

HERRINGBONE STITCH

The herringbone stitch, with its pairs of beads that slant in different directions, got its name from its resemblance to fish bones. It is an extremely popular stitch because of its pattern and versatility: in addition to flat herringbone, there are also tubular, twisted and circular versions of this stitch.

BASIC

Cell phone strap

Tubular herringbone stitch is an ideal choice for these straps because it is sturdy and pliant. The combination of seed and bugle beads adds interest and movement, and makes the work go quickly. Why not try creating your own personal color scheme? You could change colors every row or alternate colors. The possibilities are endless.

Bracelet

Like the basic strap, this bracelet is made in tubular herringbone
stitch. The number of stitches is the same throughout. We changed
only the sizes of beads. The sections made with drop beads look a lot
like bead balls. It's fun just thinking about which beads to combine for
this piece.

Instructions

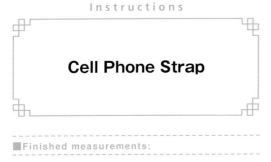

Cell Phone Strap

■Finished measurements:

0.5cm W x 19cm L (Herringbone stitch: 16cm)

■Supplies

2.2m beading thread

60 2-mm (11/0) seed beads in Color A (dark brown)

107 2-mm (11/0) seed beads in Color B (gold-lined translucent)

100 2-mm (11/0) seed beads in Color C (light brown)

32 6-mm bugle beads (gold)

2 3-mm bicone crystal beads (burgundy)

2 4-mm bicone crystal beads (burgundy)

2 6-mm round crystal beads (burgundy)

Note: Colors in parentheses are for brown strap.

1 Weave strap in tubular herringbone stitch.

❶ Work Round 1 using a technique called "ladder stitch." Attach a stopper bead to thread, leaving a 20-cm end. Add 2 seed beads in Color A. Pass through those 2 beads, working in the same direction. Pull thread to position beads as indicated in drawing (Fig. 1).

❷ Repeat Step ①, adding one seed bead in Color A, until you have 4 ladder stitches (Figs. 2 and 3).

❸ Form a ring, and pass up through first seed bead, doun through fourth bead, and then up the first bead again and step up position your needle for Round 2, referring to drawing (Fig. 4).

❹ Now weave in herringbone stitch: string 2 seed beads in Color B. Pass through second bead in previous round from above, then pass through third seed bead from below (Fig. 5).

❺ Following same procedure, add 2 seed beads in Color B, then pass through fourth bead in previous round. After completing round, pass through beads from Rounds 1 and 2, from below. Position needle for Round 3 (Fig. 6).

❻ Starting in Round 3, use colors and beads indicated in drawing, and going down to previous round to prepare for next round (Fig. 7).

❼ Pass through beads from last round only, working around tube as shown in drawing (Fig. 8).

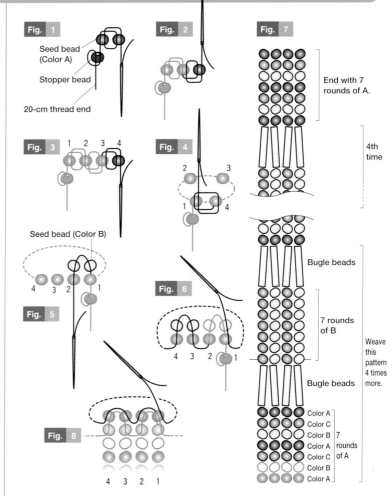

2 Attach strap finding to tube.

❶ On same thread, string a 6-mm crystal bead, a seed bead in Color C, a 4-mm crystal bead, another seed bead in Color C and a 3-mm crystal bead. Then add

11 seed beads in Color B and ring of strap finding. Pass through first seed bead added to form a loop. Add same types of crystal and seed beads, but in reverse order. Remove stopper bead at beginning of work and close circle as shown in drawing. Pass needle through beads to end of work (Fig. 9).

❷ Pass through beads again, referring to drawing, for added strength (Fig. 10).

❸ Pass needle through beads in tube. Finish off thread, making half-hitch knots as you go along and referring to drawing (Fig. 11).

❹ Finish off thread at beginning of work in same way (Fig. 12).

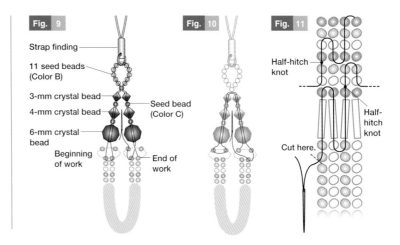

Fig. 9
Strap finding
11 seed beads (Color B)
3-mm crystal bead
4-mm crystal bead
Seed bead (Color C)
6-mm crystal bead
Beginning of work
End of work

Fig. 10

Fig. 11
Half-hitch knot
Half-hitch knot
Cut here.

Bracelet

■ **Finished measurements:**

0.5-1.5cm W x 19.5cm L

■ **Supplies**

4m beading thread
342 1.6-mm cylinder beads (light brown)
50 1.6-mm triangle beads (blue-green)
44 1.6-mm triangle beads (purple)
48 3-mm seed beads (matte dark green)
42 3-mm seed beads (matte purple)
42 3-mm seed beads (cream)
24 4-mm round fire-polished beads (pale blue)
52 4×6-mm drop beads (purple)

❶ Cut thread into two 2-m lengths. String a stopper bead on thread, leaving a 40-cm end. Make 4 ladder stitches, adding 2 cylinder beads each time. Close circle (Fig. 1).

❷ Weave Round 2 in herringbone stitch: string 2 cylinder beads, and pass through beads from previous row. After working one round, pass through 3 seed beads from Rounds 1 and 2; begin Round 3 (Fig. 6).

❸ Weave Round 3 and following rounds, passing through beads from preceding round and referring to drawing (Fig. 4). When only 20cm thread remains on needle, join new thread, making half-hitch knots as you go along (Fig. 5).

❹ When you finish the last round, make closure: passing through beads from previous round, add drop beads between stitches. End by passing needle through drop beads again. Pass needle through beads in bracelet; finish off thread (Fig. 6).

❺ Remove stopper bead at beginning of work. Add beads, referring to drawing, to make loop half of closure. Finish off thread (Fig. 7).

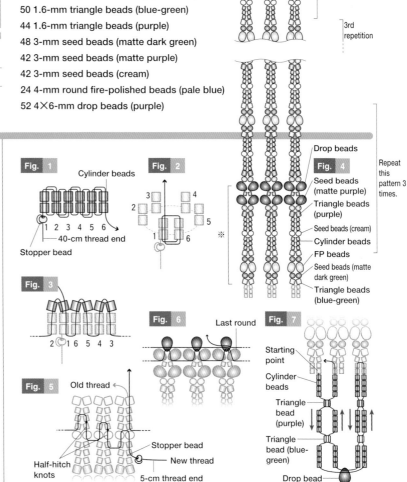

End with ※ color scheme.

3rd repetition

Repeat this pattern 3 times.

Drop beads
Seed beads (matte purple)
Triangle beads (purple)
Seed beads (cream)
Cylinder beads
FP beads
Seed beads (matte dark green)
Triangle beads (blue-green)

Fig. 1
Cylinder beads
1 2 3 4 5 6
40-cm thread end
Stopper bead

Fig. 2
3 ... 4
2 ... 5
1 ... 6

Fig. 3
2 1 6 5 4 3

Fig. 4

Fig. 5
Old thread
Half-hitch knots
Stopper bead
New thread
5-cm thread end

Fig. 6
Last round

Fig. 7
Starting point
Cylinder beads
Triangle bead (purple)
Triangle bead (blue-green)
Drop bead

NETTING

Netting, which dates back to well before the Christian era, is the stitch with the longest history. Lacy and soft, netting has lots of open areas. It can be woven both vertically and horizontally.

BASIC

Bracelet

We wove vertical netting to create this supple, diamond-patterned bracelet, which adjusts to fit your wrist perfectly. With its considerable width and all-black design, this bracelet has real presence.

Necklace

Like the basic bracelet, this necklace is woven
vertically in the netting stitch. Colors and bead
types are varied as the piece fans out, creating a
striking pattern. The red crystal and seed beads
are arranged for maximum effect.

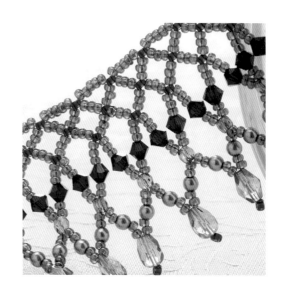

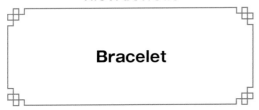

Bracelet

■**Finished measurements:**

3cm W x 18cm L (Netting: 15.5cm L)

■**Supplies**

2m beading thread
504 2-mm (11/0) seed beads (black)
80 3-mm round beads (black)
10-mm round bead (black)

1 │ Weave bracelet in netting stitch.

❶ String a stopper bead on thread, leaving a 40-cm end. Add 3-mm round beads and seed beads, referring to drawing. Pass through a round bead (Fig. 1).

❷ Add more seed beads and 3-mm round beads, referring to drawing. Pass through first round bead strung, then add more seed beads and round beads (Fig. 2).

❸ Pass through a round bead, and add seed beads and round beads. Pass through a round bead in Row 1. Add more seed beads and 3-mm round beads (Fig. 3).

❹ Weave a total of 19 rows of netting, working in the same way (Fig. 4).

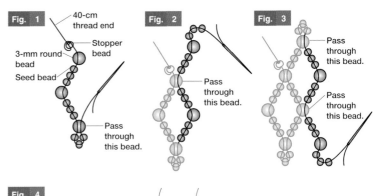

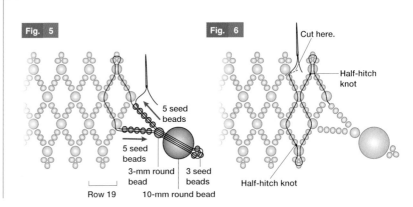

Row 1   Row 2   Row 19

2 │ Finish off thread and attach closure.

❶ Add 5 seed beads, a 3-mm round bead, 10-mm round bead and 3 more seed beads. Pass needle back through 10-mm and 3-mm round beads. Add 5 seed beads. Pass needle through beads in bracelet and closure, referring to drawing (Fig. 5).

❷ Pass needle back into bracelet, passing through beads indicated in drawing. Finish off thread, making 2-3 half-hitch knots as you go along (Fig. 6).

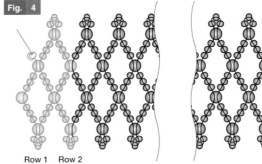

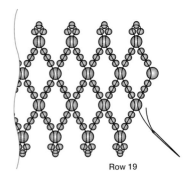

Row 19   10-mm round bead

❸ Remove stopper bead at beginning of work (★ in drawing). String 5 seed beads, a 3-mm round bead, and 22 seed beads. Pass through round bead to form a loop. Add 5 more seed beads, then pass needle through beads in bracelet, referring to drawing. Make sure loop will accommodate other half of closure. Add or subtract seed beads if necessary (Fig. 7).

❹ Pass needle back into beads in bracelet and finish off thread (Fig. 8).

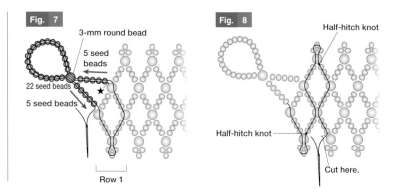

Fig. 7
3-mm round bead
5 seed beads
22 seed beads
★
5 seed beads
Row 1

Fig. 8
Half-hitch knot
Half-hitch knot
Cut here.

Instructions

Necklace

■ Finished measurements:

4cm W x 42cm L (Netting: 40cm L)

■ Supplies

6m beading thread
1,778 2-mm (11/0) seed beads (green)
201 2-mm (11/0) seed beads (red)
100 4-mm bicone crystal beads (red)
50 5 x 6-mm teardrop fire-polished beads (lavender)
51 3-mm round fire-polished beads (purple)
10-mm round fire-polished bead (red)
100 3-mm glass pearl beads (light red)

---

❶ Cut thread into 2-m lengths. String a stopper bead on thread, leaving a 20-cm end. Weave in netting stitch, stringing beads as shown in drawing (Figs. 1 and 2).

❷ When only 20cm thread remains on needle, join new thread. String a stopper bead on thread, leaving a 5-cm end. Begin using new thread at location indicated in drawing, making half-hitch knots as you go along. Finish off old thread after you've used the new thread for at least 3 rows. Weave 50 rows of netting (Fig. 3).

❸ Make closure: string 5 green seed beads, 10-mm fire-polished bead, and 3 more green fire-polished beads on thread. Pass through fire-polished bead and 5 seed beads. Pass through beads in necklace and in closure, referring to drawing. Pass needle back into beads in necklace and finish off thread (Fig. 4).

❹ Remove stopper bead at beginning of work. String 25 seed beads. Pass through first seed bead strung to form a loop. Pass through beads in necklace as indicated in drawing, then pass needle through beads in loop again. Pass needle back into beads in necklace and finish off thread (Fig. 5).

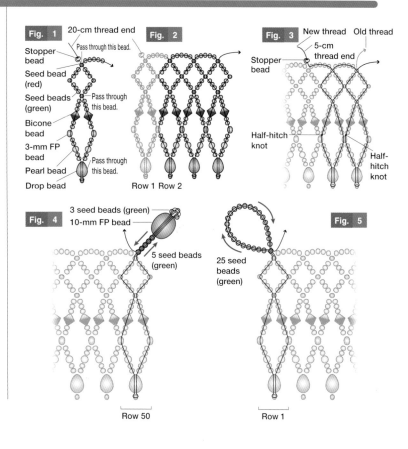

Fig. 1
20-cm thread end
Pass through this bead.
Stopper bead
Seed bead (red)
Seed beads (green)
Pass through this bead.
Bicone bead
3-mm FP bead
Pearl bead
Pass through this bead.
Drop bead

Fig. 2
Row 1 Row 2

Fig. 3
New thread Old thread
5-cm thread end
Stopper bead
Half-hitch knot
Half-hitch knot

Fig. 4
3 seed beads (green)
10-mm FP bead
5 seed beads (green)
Row 50

Fig. 5
25 seed beads (green)
Row 1

BRICK STITCH

As its name implies, brick stitch resembles a wall built from tiny bricks. If peyote stitch were turned 90 degrees, it would look like brick stitch. To work this stitch, you don't pass through beads in the previous row, but working threads. Normally, beaders weave a ladder-stitch foundation (one row) and then begin working in brick stitch.

Earrings

BASIC

These brick-stitch earrings swing gently every time you move your head. Their triangular pattern is created by increasing one stitch on each row. Framing the motifs with metal beads gives the earrings an ethereal look, while the color combinations, usually found in ethnic jewelry, make the overall impression a casual one.

Pendant

The pendant is made of five brick-stitch separate motifs, which are then joined. The five motifs have the same number of stitches as the basic earrings, but for the pendant, we varied bead types and sizes to achieve a nuanced difference. For a different effect, you might want to try using translucent beads inside the motifs.

Instructions

Earrings

■Finished measurements:

4.5cm L (Motifs: 1.2cm W x 1.2cm L)

■Supplies

4.2m beading thread

40 1.6-mm cylinder beads in Color A (matte gold/pale blue)

27 1.6-mm cylinder beads in Color B (yellow-green/rust)

22 1.6-mm cylinder beads in Color C (yellow/purple)

132 1.5-mm (15/0) seed beads (bronze/bronze)

6 3-mm bicone crystal beads (olive/lavender)

6 4-mm bicone crystal beads (olive/lavender)

Earring backs

1 Weave brick-stitch motif.

❶ Cut a 50-cm length of thread. Weave Motif A: string 2 cylinder beads in Color A on thread, leaving a 20-cm end. Pass through same 2 beads again, working in same direction, and pull thread. Pass through first bead strung (Fig. 1).

❷ Weave Row 2: string one cylinder bead in Color A and one in Color B. Pass through working thread in Row 1 from the back. Then pass through a bead in color B from underneath (Fig. 2).

❸ Add a cylinder bead in Color A. Pass through same working thread in previous row again. Then pass through a bead in Color A from underneath. You have completed two rows (Fig. 3).

❹ Continue in the same way, adding a bead at each edge, until you have 6 rows. For the first stitch on each row you will be adding 2 beads; elsewhere, one bead (Figs. 4 and 5).

❺ String a seed bead on top of each bead in last row, passing through working threads in last row, as shown in drawing (Fig. 6).

❻ Finish off thread: pass needle back into motif in a diagonal pattern (see drawing), and cut thread at edge of a bead. Finish off thread at beginning of work in the same way (Fig. 7).

❼ Cut two 80-cm lengths of thread and weave two of Motif A', leaving a 50-cm thread end. Set thread at beginning of work aside.

2 Join motifs and attach earring backs.

❶ String a 3-mm bicone bead, seed beads, cylinder beads and 4-mm bicone bead on thread end at beginning of Motif A', as shown in drawing. Pass through same beads, then pass needle through beads in motif and finish off thread (Fig. 8).

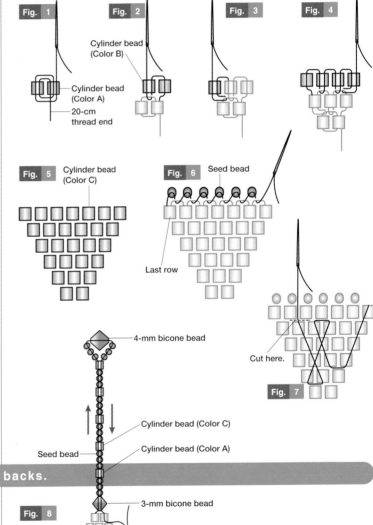

Fig. 1

Fig. 2
Cylinder bead (Color B)
Cylinder bead (Color A)
20-cm thread end

Fig. 3

Fig. 4

Fig. 5
Cylinder bead (Color C)

Fig. 6
Seed bead
Last row

Cut here.

Fig. 7

4-mm bicone bead

Cylinder bead (Color C)
Cylinder bead (Color A)
Seed bead

3-mm bicone bead

Fig. 8
Motif A'

❷ On thread extending from beginning of other Motif A', string a 3-mm bicone bead, seed beads, and cylinder beads. Pass through seed bead and 4-mm bicone bead strung in Step ①, referring to drawing. Add a seed bead, a 4-mm bicone bead, 10 more seed beads, and ring on earring back. Pass through first seed bead to form a loop. Pass needle through 4-mm bicone bead and seed beads strung in Step ① again (Fig. 9).

❸ String seed beads, cylinder beads and a 3-mm crystal bead, referring to drawing. Pass through beads in Motif A to join. Then pass through beads indicated in drawing to strengthen the loop. Pass needle through beads in Motif A' at right and finish off thread (Fig. 10).

❹ Make other earring in same way.

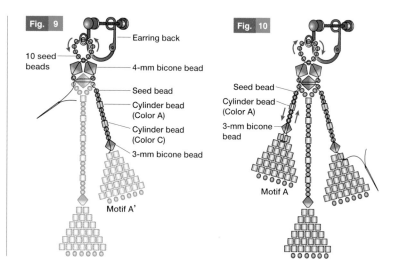

Fig. 9
Earring back
10 seed beads
4-mm bicone bead
Seed bead
Cylinder bead (Color A)
Cylinder bead (Color C)
3-mm bicone bead
Motif A'

Fig. 10
Seed bead
Cylinder bead (Color A)
3-mm bicone bead
Motif A

Instructions

Pendant

■Finished length:

7.5cm L (pendant only)

■Supplies

5m beading thread

12 6-mm bugle beads in Color A (blue-green)

9 6-mm bugle beads in Color B (matte silver)

6 6-mm bugle beads in Color C (orange)

12 4-mm cube beads in Color A (blue-green)

9 4-mm cube beads in Color B (matte silver)

6 4-mm cube beads in Color C (orange)

13 3-mm (8/0) seed beads in Color A (blue-green)

9 3-mm (8/0) seed beads in Color B (matte silver)

7 3-mm (8/0) seed beads in Color C (orange)

16 2-mm (11/0) seed beads in Color A (blue-green)

27 2-mm (11/0) seed beads in Color B (matte silver)

7 2-mm (11/0) seed beads in Color C (orange)

61 2-mm (11/0) seed beads in Color D (light gold)

❶ Cut thread into 75-cm lengths. You will be making 5 motifs in brick stitch. Leaving a 30-cm thread end, weave 6 rows in color scheme indicated in drawings. Finish off thread at end of each motif (Figs. 1-7).

❷ On thread end at beginning of Motif A, string 2-mm and 3-mm seed beads, referring to drawing. Pass needle through beads again, then beads in motif. Finish off thread (Fig. 8).

❸ On thread end at beginning of Motif B, string 2-mm seed beads, referring to drawing. Join to Motif A. Pass needle through beads in loop again, then through beads in motif. Finish off thread (Fig. 9).

❹ Join Motifs C, D and E in the same way (Fig. 10).

❺ Make necklace with beads of your choosing. Thread necklace through loop on pendant.

15 2-mm seed beads (Color D)
3-mm seed bead (Color A)
3-mm seed bead (Color C)

Fig. 1
Bugle bead (Color A)
30-cm thread end

Fig. 2
Bugle bead (Color B)

Fig. 3
Bugle bead (Color C)
Motif A

Fig. 4
Cube bead (Color C)
Cube bead (Color B)
Cube bead (Color A)
Motif B

Fig. 5
3-mm seed bead (Color C)
3-mm seed bead (Color B)
3-mm seed bead (Color A)
Motif C

Fig. 6
2-mm seed bead (Color A) Motif D

Fig. 7
2-mm seed bead (Color B) Motif E

2-mm seed bead (Color D)

Fig. 8
2-mm seed bead (Color A)
2-mm seed bead (Color D)
2-mm seed bead (Color C)
Motif A

Fig. 9
2-mm seed bead (Color A)
4 2-mm seed beads (Color D)
2-mm seed bead (Color C)
Motif B

Fig. 10
2-mm seed bead (Color D)
2-mm seed bead (Color A)
2-mm seed bead (Color C)
Motif D
Motif C
Motif E

RIGHT-ANGLE WEAVE

This stitch got its name because the woven beads sit at right angles to each other. It could also be called the figure-eight stitch, since the thread makes a figure-eight path among the beads. This stitch creates an open, lacy pattern that lends itself well to embellishment.

Bracelet

BASIC

This gorgeous, wide bracelet consists of three rows of right-angle weave stitch made with bugle and seed beads. The fire-polished beads and tiny seed beads are accents added afterwards. Using other accent beads will, of course, produce a different effect.

Choker

Like the basic bracelet, this elegant two-row choker is woven in right-angle weave with bugle and seed beads, and decorated afterwards with fire-polished beads and tiny seed beads. After you're finished weaving, simply thread a length of ribbon through the loop at each end of the choker.

Instructions

Bracelet

Finished length:

17.5cm L (Right-angle weave: 14.5cm)

Supplies

4m beading thread

164 3-mm bugle beads (white)

276 2-mm (11/0) seed beads (milky white)

138 1.5-mm (15/0) seed beads (silver)

46 4-mm round fire-polished beads (milky white)

23 5-mm round fire-polished beads (transparent)

8 x 20-mm Czech barrel bead (milky white)

1 Weave band of bracelet in right-angle weave.

❶ Cut a 2.4-m length of thread. String a stopper bead on thread, leaving a 20-cm end. String bugle and 2-mm seed beads, referring to drawing. Pass through first 5 bugle beads strung and pull thread. You now have one right-angle weave stitch (Figs. 1 and 2).

❷ String 2-mm seed beads and bugle beads, referring to drawing, and pass up through last bugle bead in first stitch to close square shape. Pass up through first 4 beads in second stitch (Fig. 3).

❸ Continue in the same way until you have 23 right-angle weave stitches. After closing the circle on the last stitch, pass through 2 beads (Fig. 4).

❹ Weave Row 2: string 2-mm seed beads and bugle beads, referring to drawing. Pass through last bugle bead in Row 1 to close circle. Pass through more beads, again referring to drawing. Weave 23 stitches, passing through bugle beads in Row 1 (Fig. 5).

❺ Row 3: work in the same way as Step (2), making 23 stitches (Fig. 6).

❻ Finish off thread: pass needle back through beads, referring to drawing; make 2-3 half-hitch knots as you go along. Cut excess thread at edge of a bead. Remove stopper bead at beginning of work (★ in drawing) and finish off thread in same way (Fig. 7).

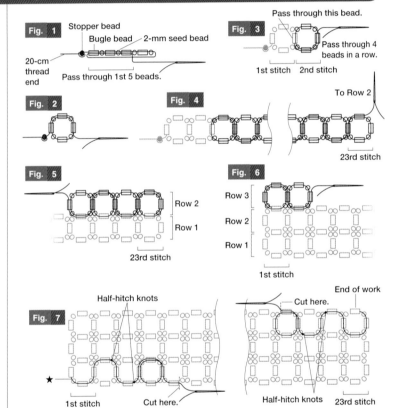

Fig. 1 — Stopper bead / Bugle bead / 2-mm seed bead / 20-cm thread end / Pass through 1st 5 beads.

Fig. 3 — Pass through this bead. / Pass through 4 beads in a row. / 1st stitch / 2nd stitch / To Row 2

Fig. 2

Fig. 4 — 23rd stitch

Fig. 5 — Row 2 / Row 1 / 23rd stitch

Fig. 6 — Row 3 / Row 2 / Row 1 / 1st stitch

Fig. 7 — Half-hitch knots / Cut here. / End of work / ★ / 1st stitch / Cut here. / Half-hitch knots / 23rd stitch

2 Decorate the right-angle weave and attach closure.

❶ Cut a 1.6-m length of thread. String a stopper bead, leaving a 30-cm end. Pass through the bugle bead at right edge of Row 1 from underneath. Add a 1.5-mm seed bead, a 4-mm fire-polished bead and another 1.5-mm seed bead. Pass through bugle bead indicated in drawing. Repeat until you reach left edge of Row 1 (Fig. 8).

❷ Pass through bugle bead in last stitch of Row 1 from the bottom, referring to drawing, and proceed to Row 2. Pass needle through all beads in first stitch of Row 2. Add a 1.5-mm seed bead, a 5-mm fire-polished bead and another 1.5-mm seed bead, then pass through a bugle bead. Repeat until you reach right edge of Row 2 (Fig. 9).

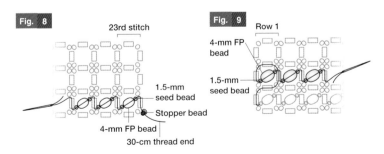

Fig. 8 — 23rd stitch / 1.5-mm seed bead / Stopper bead / 4-mm FP bead / 30-cm thread end

Fig. 9 — Row 1 / 4-mm FP bead / 1.5-mm seed bead

❸ Pass needle through beads in last stitch of Row 2, then proceed to Row 3. Work as directed in Step ① until you reach left edge (Fig. 10).

❹ Using same thread, pass needle through bugle bead in first stitch, then string beads for closure, referring to drawing (Fig. 11).

❺ Pass needle through beads in bracelet, as shown in drawing, and then through closure beads once again. Pass needle back through beads in bracelet and finish off thread (Fig. 12).

❻ Remove stopper bead at beginning of work. String beads on thread, referring to drawing, and forming a loop (Fig. 13).

❼ Pass through beads in bracelet, as shown in drawing. Pass needle through beads in loop once again. Finish off thread (Fig. 14).

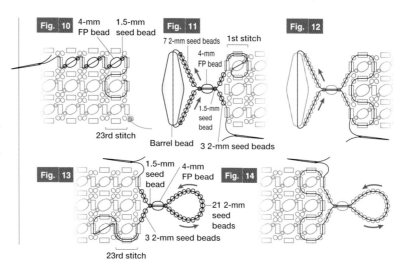

Fig. 10 — 4-mm FP bead — 1.5-mm seed bead — 23rd stitch
Fig. 11 — 7 2-mm seed beads — 4-mm FP bead — 1st stitch — 1.5-mm seed bead — Barrel bead — 3 2-mm seed beads
Fig. 12
Fig. 13 — 1.5-mm seed bead — 4-mm FP bead — 21 2-mm seed beads — 3 2-mm seed beads — 23rd stitch
Fig. 14

Instructions

Choker

▮Finished length:

1.5cm W x 19cm L (woven portion)

▮Supplies

3.8m beading thread

236 2-mm (11/0) seed beads (light reddish gold)

28 4-mm round fire-polished beads (rose)

28 4-mm round fire-polished beads (light brown)

142 6-mm bugle beads (gold)

126 1.5-mm (15/0) seed beads (gold)

1m 1-cm ribbon (brown)

❶ Cut a 2.2-m length of thread. String a stopper bead on thread, leaving a 20-cm end. Weave 28 right-angle weave stitches with bugle and 2-mm seed beads, referring to drawing. After closing the circle, pass through 6 beads and proceed to Row 2 (Fig. 1).

❷ Weave Row 2, referring to drawing. Set thread aside. Remove stopper bead at beginning of work and finish off thread (Fig. 2).

❸ Decorate the right-angle weave stitches: cut a 1.6-m length of thread. String a stopper bead, leaving a 20-cm end. Pass through bugle bead at right edge of Row 1 from underneath. Add 1.5-mm seed beads and a rose fire-polished bead to each stitch in row. For Row 2, add 1.5-mm seed beads and a light-brown fire-polished bead. Bring thread out from bugle bead at right edge (Fig. 3).

❹ Pass through adjacent 2-mm seed bead, then add 1.5-mm and 2-mm seed beads in alternation to form a loop. Pass needle back into beads in choker, then through beads in loop again. Finish off thread (Fig. 4).

❺ Thread needle with thread set aside in Step ②. Pass through adjacent 2-mm seed bead. Repeat Step ④ to form a loop. Finish off thread (Fig. 5).

❻ Thread ribbon through loops.

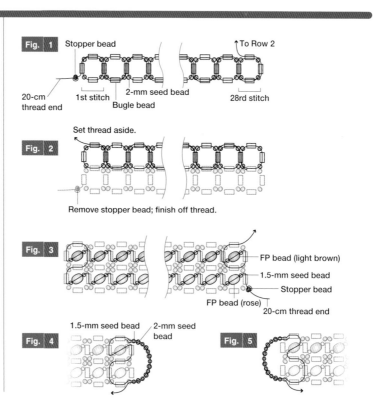

Fig. 1 — Stopper bead — To Row 2 — 20-cm thread end — 1st stitch — 2-mm seed bead — Bugle bead — 28rd stitch
Fig. 2 — Set thread aside. — Remove stopper bead; finish off thread.
Fig. 3 — FP bead (light brown) — 1.5-mm seed bead — Stopper bead — FP bead (rose) — 20-cm thread end
Fig. 4 — 1.5-mm seed bead — 2-mm seed bead
Fig. 5

BASIC TOOLS AND SUPPLIES

Tools and Supplies

You don't need to assemble a lot of equipment or supplies. That's part of what makes this type of beadwork so attractive. To start out, all you need are beading thread, beading needles, and beads. You can acquire other tools when necessary.

Beading needles

You'll be passing your needle through the same beads any number of times, so you need a very thin needle. It should also be flexible, since you'll need to pass through beads that aren't facing in the same direction.

✳ Needle length

Beading needles come in several lengths ranging from 3cm to 5cm. Longer needles are convenient when you need to string a lot of beads at once. Most beaders use the long needles, but the shorter needles come in handy when you're finishing off thread or passing through one bead in the middle of a woven piece.

✳ Needle thickness

The needles most commonly used are sizes 10, 11 and 12 (the larger the number, the finer the needle). We recommend Size 10 to beginners because it has a large hole and is easy to work with.

Miss Pyramis beading needles from Toho Beads

PEERLONE beading needles from Tulip Co.

Beading needles in an assortment of lengths from Clover

Beading needles from the British firm John James

Tools you'll need

Scissors
Use scissors designed for cutting thread. Patchwork scissors (bottom in photo), with their curved blades, are very useful because they won't damage beads and they're easy to maneuver when you need to cut one thread (and only one thread).

Tape measure
You'll definitely need one of these for measuring thread and woven pieces.

Beading mat
Buy a cushioned, fairly thick mat that will accommodate your needle when you're not using it. Folding mats are available, as well as tray mats like the one shown in the photo.

Other useful items

Sorting tray
These are good for sorting and storing beads and other small items.

Portable beading mat
Shaped like a carrying case, this handy mat is perfect for keeping beads and your woven piece out of harm's way when you're not beading. When it's open, you can use both halves. It comes with a bead scoop.

Magnifiers
These are very useful when you're working with tiny beads. The folding type with an attached light is good, because it doesn't take up much space.

Beeswax: Used to strengthen nylon thread.
Thread conditioner: Smooths thread and keeps it from fraying or tangling.

Beading thread

✳ Nylon thread

Many beaders use nylon thread, which is usually coated with wax. Nylon thread is fine, a quality that makes it ideal for work that involves passing the needle through the same beads any number of times. We also like nylon thread because it doesn't split easily, having no twist, and because its elasticity makes it easy to pull when you need to. ONE G beading thread, which doesn't fade or fray, and comes in a wide variety of colors, is perfect for beginners.

✳ Other synthetics

Thread made of other synthetic fibers is generally sturdier than nylon thread. Many of these threads originated as fishing line, and are therefore water-resistant. Each type has its strong points. Power Pro, a U.S. brand, is on the thick side, and very easy to work with. FireLine, also a U.S. brand, is thin, but tough and just as easy to work with.

Commonly used beads

Seed beads
These small cylindrical beads range in size from 1.5mm to 4mm. In Europe and the U.S., these beads are classified by numbers like 8/0 for 3-mm diameter or 11/0 for 2-mm diameter (the higher the number, the smaller the bead), or by diameter measurement in millimeters, or both.

Cylinder beads
Shaped like tiny cylinders, these beads have large holes and are amazingly uniform in size. Because of this characteristic, they are prized by beaders who do loom work. Depending on the stitch, of course, work done with these beads can feel as smooth as silk.

Polygonal beads
This class of beads includes triangle, cube and hex (hexagonal) beads. All of them have round holes.

Bugle beads
The most common sizes of these long cylindrical beads are 3mm and 6mm.

Fire-polished beads
Polished over an open fire, these beads have rounded facets and a special luster.

Crystal beads
The most famous manufacturer of these faceted beads is the Austrian firm Swarovski. Bicone and round crystal beads are shown in the photo.

Pearl beads
Both natural pearl beads (including freshwater pearl beads) and glass imitations are available.

Drop beads
Also called teardrop beads, these get their name from their shape.

Findings

Bar-and-ring toggle closure
This is one of many types of closures. You close it by inserting the bar half into the ring half.

Earring backs
Earring backs for unpierced ears come in two types: clip-on backs and screw backs. The findings in the photo are screw backs.

BASIC STITCH MAPS

Peyote stitch

■ Flat peyote stitch (even-count)

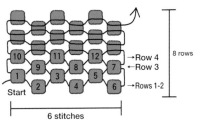

6 stitches

Beads for Rows 1 and 2 are strung at the same time. In Row 3, string a new bead, skip a bead on the previous row, and pass through the next one. Starting with Row 4, pass through the beads that protrude from the preceding row.

■ Flat peyote stitch (odd-count)

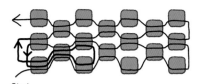

Start

When you have no next bead to go to, you will need to make turns in some of the beads already strung so that you can start the next row.

■ Making a one-stitch increase at an edge

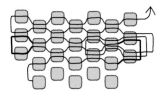

String 2 beads at the edge.

■ Making a one-stitch decrease at an edge

Make turns as you would with odd-count peyote stitch. The thread should go into the bead at the edge on the diagonal.

■ Circular peyote stitch (making an increase)

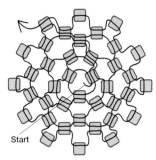

Start

String 2 beads where you wish to make the increase. On the next row, pass through these 2 beads separately.

■ Circular peyote stitch (making a decrease)

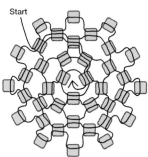

Start

Pass through 2 beads at the same time where you wish to make the decrease. On the next row, string only one bead.

■ Tubular peyote stitch (even-count) step up

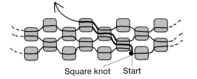

Square knot   Start

To prepare for the next row, pass needle through first bead picked up in row and first bead strung.

■ Tubular peyote stitch: odd-count (spiral)

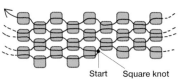

Start   Square knot

There is no "step up" for odd-count tubular peyote stitch.

Ladder stitch

■ One-bead ladder stitch

Start

Ladder stitch is often used at the beginning of brick and herringbone-stitch weaving.

■ Two-bead ladder stitch

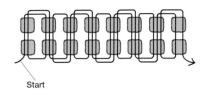

Start

Brick stitch

■ Flat brick stitch (ladder-stitch beginning)

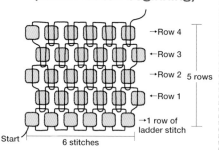

→Row 4
←Row 3
→Row 2   5 rows
←Row 1
→1 row of ladder stitch

Start   6 stitches

Weave 1 row of ladder stitch. Pass through working threads, not beads. String 2 beads at beginning.

■ Making a one-stitch increase at an edge

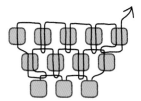

On the edge where you began work, string 2 beads and pass through working thread between last 2 beads on previous row.
On opposite edge, pass through first working thread twice.

■ Making a one-stitch decrease at an edge

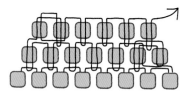

On the edge where you began work, string 2 beads, then pass through second working thread. Work as in ladder stitch (down and back up through beads) to straighten and stabilize beads. On opposite edge, string one bead and pass through last working thread.

Herringbone stitch

■ Flat herringbone stitch

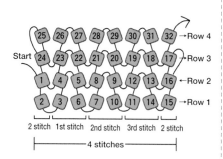

25 26 27 28 29 30 31 32 →Row 4
Start 24 23 22 21 20 19 18 17 →Row 3
1 4 5 8 9 12 13 16 ←Row 2
2 3 6 7 10 11 14 15 →Row 1

2 stitch 1st stitch 2nd stitch 3rd stitch 2 stitch
← 4 stitches →

String beads for Rows 1 and 2 all at once. Work in pattern starting with Row 3. You will have a half stitch at each edge.

■ Flat herringbone stitch (ladder-stitch beginning)

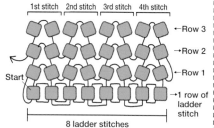

1st stitch 2nd stitch 3rd stitch 4th stitch
←Row 3
→Row 2
←Row 1
→1 row of ladder stitch

Start

8 ladder stitches
(twice the number of herringbone stitches)

Weave one row of ladder stitch.
You will have whole stitches at the edges.

■ Tubular herringbone stitch step up (herringbone stitch beginning)

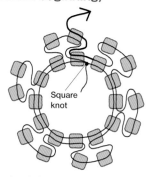

Square knot

String beads for first row. Join first and last beads to close circle. Work in herringbone stitch starting with Row 2.

■ Tubular spiral herringbone stitch

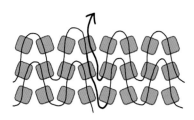

Weave in a spiral pattern. There is no step up for this stitch.

■ Circular herringbone stitch

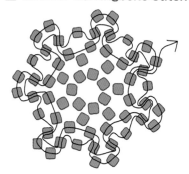

Weave first 3 rows in peyote stitch.

■ Tubular herringbone stitch step up (ladder-stitch beginning)

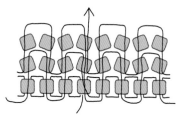

Work first row in ladder stitch. Switch to herringbone stitch in Row 2.

Netting

■ Flat netting (vertical)

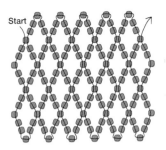

Start

Thread is perpendicular to the direction in which the work progresses.

■ Flat netting (horizontal)

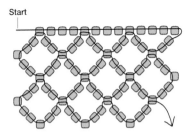

Start

Thread is parallel to the direction in which the work progresses.

Square stitch

■ Flat square stitch

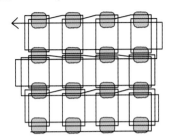

After completing a row, pass needle through beads in previous row and row just completed.

Right-angle weave stitch

■ Flat right-angle weave (even-count)

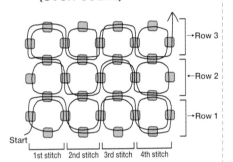

Row 3
Row 2
Row 1

Start

1st stitch   2nd stitch   3rd stitch   4th stitch

String 4 beads to form a circle, then pass through 2 of them again. Starting with the 2nd stitch, string 3 beads at a time. In Row 2, connect new stitches to stitches in preceding row.

■ Flat right-angle weave stitch (odd-count)

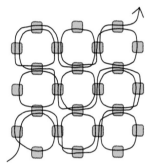

After working the last stitch, pass through only the last bead added, then begin next row.

Spiral rope stitch

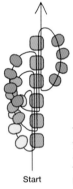

Start

To work this stitch, you wrap outer beads around core beads to form a spiral. Outer beads can be wrapped either to the left or right, as long as you stick to one direction.

Daisy chain stitch

■ Open daisy chain stitch

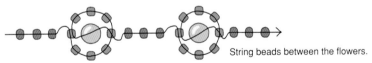

String beads between the flowers.

■ Continuous daisy chain stitch connected by one bead

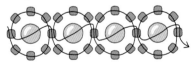

Adjacent daisies have one "petal" in common.

■ Continuous daisy chain stitch connected by 2 beads

Adjacent daisies have two "petals" in common.

BONUS SECTION ON
PEYOTE STITCH

CONTENTS

Peyote stitch is immensely popular, the most popular of all beading stitches because it is easy to work and offers endless possibilities.

Peyote Stitch

The seeds on the peyote plant are reminiscent of the pattern formed by peyote stitch.

Introduction

Among the beading stitches introduced in this book, peyote stitch is the technique most commonly used. Native Americans use the peyote stitch to create beadwork that decorates ceremonial objects. The name "peyote stitch" comes from the resemblance of the pattern the stitch creates to the peyote plant, a type of cactus used in religious ceremonies.

Peyote stitch is quite simple. All you do is string a bead where there's a valley between two "peaks" in the preceding row, and then pass through a bead from the next peak. Because the pattern formed by peyote stitch is quite regular, resembling rows of tiny bricks, you'll find that it adapts well to charts.

The Native Americans use peyote stitch primarily to create covers and containers for objects. In contemporary beadwork, the most commonly used versions of the stitch are flat peyote, tubular peyote, and circular peyote stitch.

The most basic (and easiest) type of peyote stitch is flat, odd-count peyote stitch. This is typically the first stitch attempted by beginners. Also very accessible is tubular peyote stitch, which forms a tube, just as the name suggests. It can also form a spiral if you vary bead sizes; this stitch is ideal for necklaces and bracelets.

By making increases as you work, you can create flat squares or circles. Since it's easy to make increases or decreases, you can create an amazing range of variations, for instance, a frame for a cabochon, or frills.

We also recommend peyote stitch for three-dimensional pieces, since it holds its shape so well.

Native Americans use peyote-stitch decorations like this one to cover tools used in religious ceremonies. (Design and execution: Yoshie Marubashi)

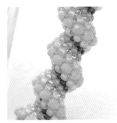

Necklace made with tubular peyote stitch (Lesson 3)

Box worked in three-dimensional peyote stitch (Lesson 4)

Pendant made with circular peyote stitch (Lesson 5)

Cell-phone strap worked in flat, odd-count peyote stitch (Lesson 6)

Brooch worked in flat peyote stitch with gradual decreases (Lesson 6)

Lesson * 1

Make a bracelet while learning peyote stitch.

Here you'll be making a bracelet with flat peyote stitch, while you get accustomed to basic techniques like passing through beads and finishing off thread. If this is the first project you're attempting in this book, please take the time to read the introductory material at the beginning.

Spring Blossom Bracelet

Design: Kimie Suto

To make this bracelet, you weave four motifs in flat peyote stitch, which you then join. The pastel colors used in the bracelet and the little garlands between motifs are sure to remind you of the flowers that are so welcome in spring.

Spring Blossom Bracelet

▓Supplies

3.2m beading thread
127 3-mm (8/0) seed beads (cream)
96 3-mm (8/0) seed beads (lavender)
73 2-mm (11/0) seed beads (cream)
108 2-mm (11/0) seed beads (lavender)
6 7-mm designer flower beads (cream)
6 7-mm designer flower beads (pink)
6 7-mm designer flower beads (green)
23-mm gemstone flower bead (pink)
4-mm glass pearl bead (white)

▓Finished measurements:

1cm W x 19cm L (before garland accents are twisted)

---

1 Read instructions.

First make 4 rectangular motifs (A-D) in peyote stitch. Finish off thread at end of Motifs B, C and D. Join motifs while adding decorative beads. Attach closure to one end and loop to other.

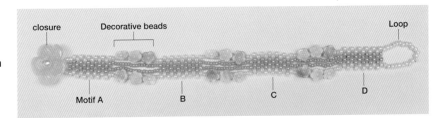

closure   Decorative beads   Loop

Motif A   B   C   D

---

2 Weave 4 motifs in flat peyote stitch.

1 Cut an 80-cm length of thread; string a stopper bead on thread.

Cut 80cm thread for motif. After you thread your needle, string a (temporary) stopper bead on thread, leaving a 30-cm end.

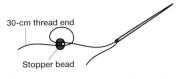

30-cm thread end

Stopper bead

❶ String a stopper bead on thread 30cm from end; pass needle through bead again, moving in same direction.

❷ Pull thread to stabilize stopper bead (thread in drawing has been shortened to save space).

TIP

A stopper bead is placed at one end of the thread to keep beads from falling off. It is removed once a piece is finished. We recommend choosing a 2-mm (11/0) seed bead of a very different color than the other beads you'll be using. Placement of the stopper differs with each piece.

2 Make Motif A in peyote stitch.

The basics of flat peyote stitch involve adding a new bead, skipping a bead, and passing through a high bead.

You repeat this procedure, going back and forth from left to right, to the left again, etc. The sides of your woven piece will be straight, but the first bead will protrude, while the last one will be recessed.

12 3-mm seed beads (cream)

❶ String 12 cream 3-mm seed beads on thread. Slide them so they rest next to stopper bead. These will form the first 2 rows.

3-mm seed beads (lavender)
pass through this bead.

❷ Weave Row 3. Add a lavender 3-mm seed bead and pass through 2nd cream seed bead from right edge.

Pass through this bead.

❸ Add a lavender 3-mm seed bead, skip one cream seed bead, and pass through 2nd cream seed bead.

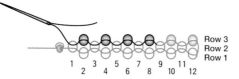

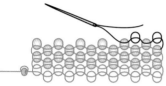

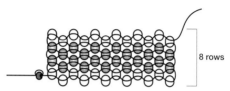

④ Repeat Step ③ 4 times. You have woven 3 12-stitch rows of peyote stitch. Beads protrude or are recessed, in alternation. Stitches and rows are counted as shown in drawing above.

⑤ For Rows 4-6, string one lavender 3-mm seed bead at a time, skip a recessed seed bead, and pass through the next protruding bead.

⑥ For Rows 7 and 8, add one cream 3-mm seed bead at a time, and pass through protruding beads in previous row.

⑦ Once you have woven Row 8, you are finished with Motif A. Set thread aside.

TIPS

■ When you pass through beads, be sure to pull the thread.

In our drawings, the beads are shown with spaces between them for instructional purposes. But you should pull on the thread while you are weaving to make sure there are no spaces between beads. Every time you pass through a bead (or beads), pull the thread so the beads line up perfectly. When you're weaving the 3rd row, your work should look like the photos at right.

Pass through 2nd 3-mm seed bead from right. Pull thread.

Pass through 4th seed bead from right. Pull thread.

■ Feel free to work with wrong side up.

In our drawings, the weaving is shown right side up so we can show you the thread path. But it's perfectly all right to work with the wrong side up.

Row 4 of wrong side of bracelet

■ Make sure you're holding your work and pulling the thread correctly.

When you pass through a bead, you should have your weaving in one hand and hold down the thread extending from it with your fingers. This way the thread won't loosen, and you'll be less likely to split it with the needle. When you pull the thread, pull it in a straight line so it doesn't rub against bead edges.

Place thread extending from work over your index finger from front to back. Hold it between your index and middle fingers.

When you're pulling a long thread, hold the needle in your hand as shown in photo, and pull thread, a little at a time, with your thumb and index finger.

3 Make Motifs B, C and D; finish off thread at beginning of work.

Make these three motifs in the same way as Motif A, except for the location of the stopper bead, which should be 20cm from the end. Set remaining thread aside. Finish off thread end at beginning of work, following directions below.

20-cm thread end

Make 3.

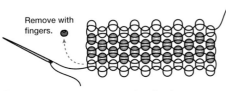

Remove with fingers.

1 Pull stopper bead off thread, going in same direction as thread. Thread needle with same thread.

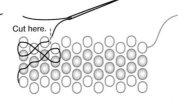

Cut here.

2 Run needle through beads in weaving, moving diagonally and turning to form intersections. Cut excess thread at edge of a bead.

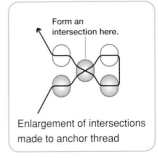

Form an intersection here.

Enlargement of intersections made to anchor thread

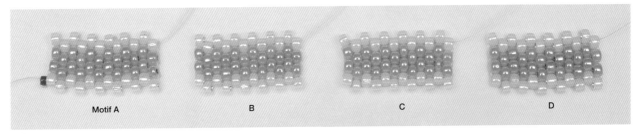

Motif A   B   C   D

3 Finish off thread at beginning of all motifs except for Motif A (do not remove stopper bead on this motif).

TIPS

■ Finish off excess thread by running needle through woven piece.

To finish of excess thread at beginning and end of a woven piece, you run the needle back through the woven piece. If the piece is flat, pass the needle diagonally through beads, turning 2-3 times to form intersections along the way. If you have trouble getting your needle through a lot of beads at once, pass through 2 or 3 beads at a time.

1 Insert needle into beads adjacent to first bead strung; pass it through more beads, moving diagonally.

2 Turn and pass needle through 4 beads (2 beads in photo), again moving diagonally.

■ Cut excess thread at edge of a bead.

Cut excess thread at the edge of a bead. Pull the thread as you cut it so thread end won't show.

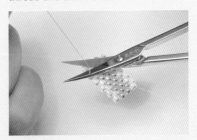

This operation is simple if you use scissors with curved blades.

3 Join 4 motifs and attach closure.

▌ Add decorative beads between motifs.

String decorative beads between motifs, using thread extending from the end of each motif, and then passing through beads from motif to join.

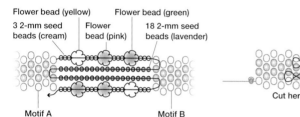

Flower bead (yellow)
Flower bead (green)
3 2-mm seed beads (cream)
Flower bead (pink)
18 2-mm seed beads (lavender)

Motif A   Motif B

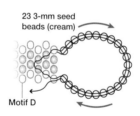

Cut here.

❶ String 2-mm seed beads and flower beads on thread extending from end of Motif A, referring to drawing. Pass through 2 3-mm seed beads in Motif B, then string 18 lavender 2-mm seed beads. Repeat this process, referring to drawing and passing through 2 3-mm seed beads in motif each time.

❷ Pass through 3-mm beads at bottom right of Motif A. Finish off thread by passing through more beads, moving on the diagonal. Add decorative beads to and join Motifs B and C, and C and D in the same way. Finish off thread.

TIP

▌ Pull thread when you add decorative beads.

Pull thread each time you add a decorative bead and pass through a 3-mm seed bead.

▨ Attach closure to Motifs A and D.

Remove stopper bead from Motif A, and string beads for closure on thread at beginning of motif. Attach a loop to end of Motif D.

▌BEGINNING OF MOTIF A

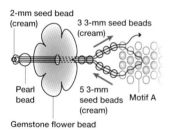

2-mm seed bead (cream)
3 3-mm seed beads (cream)
Pearl bead
5 3-mm seed beads (cream)
Motif A
Gemstone flower bead

String 5 cream 3-mm seed beads, gemstone bead, a pearl bead and a cream 2-mm seed bead on thread at beginning of motif. Pass needle through pearl and flower beads, and 2 3-mm seed beads again. Add 3 cream 3-mm seed beads. Pass through beads in motif, referring to drawing. Pass needle through beads in closure once again for added strength. Pass through beads in motif and finish off thread.

▌End of Motif D

23 3-mm seed beads (cream)
Motif D

String 23 cream 3-mm seed beads on thread at end of motif. Pass through beads in motif, referring to drawing. Pass needle through beads in loop again for added strength. Pass through beads in motif and finish off thread. Make sure the loop will accommodate other half of closure, and add or subtract seed beads if necessary.

TIP

▌ For a lovely effect, twist decorative beads.

Twisting the beads gives the bracelet an airier look.

❶ Thread the bracelet through the 2nd and 3rd strands of decorative beads.

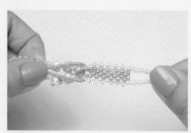

❷ Pull, then thread bracelet through decorative beads again.

❸ After the second time, decorative beads should twist as in photo above.

Make a ring while learning peyote stitch.

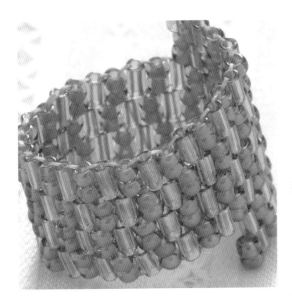

As in Lesson 1, you will be working in flat peyote stitch, this time to make a ring. You will be learning how to make two-drop peyote stitch, which adds two beads for each stitch, and how to join the edges of a woven piece to form a circle. You'll be weaving more rows to make this ring than you did for the bracelet in Lesson 1, so you might want to practice the technique first.

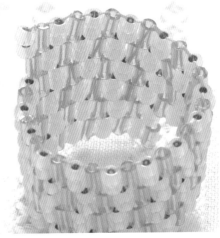

Two-drop Ring

Design: Hiroe Takagi

This simple ring is made with 2-mm seed beads and bugle beads. You'll be stringing the longer bugle beads one at a time, but the 2-mm seed beads are strung two at a time, to make what is called "two-drop" peyote stitch. You will be decreasing stitches midway, so the ring will have an angular look once the edges are joined. You can, of course, get different effects by using different types of beads or changing the number of stitches.

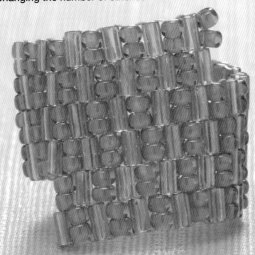

Two-Drop Ring

■Finished measurements:

12mm (diameter)

■Supplies

1.5m beading thread
154 2-mm seed beads (pink/cream)
77 3-mm bugle beads (yellow-green/pale blue)

1 Weave band in flat peyote stitch.

Weave two-drop peyote stitch (two 2-mm seed beads make one stitch). You will be weaving the same way as in Lesson 1, with the exception that you add weave 2 rows with seed beads and 2 rows of bugle beads in alternation. You will also be changing the number of stitches midway through the project.

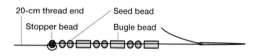

❶ String a stopper bead on thread, leaving a 20-cm end. String three sets of beads (each set has 2 seed beads and a bugle bead) to make Rows 1 and 2.

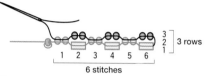

❷ String 2 seed beads and pass through 2 seed beads. Repeat for a total of 3 times. You have now woven 3 6-stitch rows of peyote stitch. Two seed beads form one stitch.

❸ On Row 4, string a bugle bead and pass through 2 seed beads.

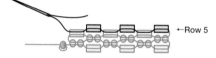

❹ On Row 5, add a bugle bead and pass through a bugle bead.

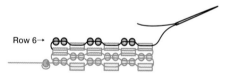

❺ On Row 6, add 2 seed beads and pass through one bugle bead.

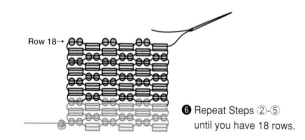

❻ Repeat Steps ②-⑤ until you have 18 rows.

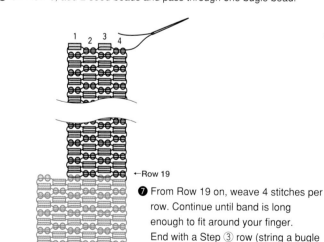

❼ From Row 19 on, weave 4 stitches per row. Continue until band is long enough to fit around your finger. End with a Step ③ row (string a bugle bead and pass through 2 seed beads). [For a Size 15 ring, figure 68 rows.]

■ Make sure the ring fits.

To make adjustments in the length of the band, you increase or decrease the number of rows. When your woven piece reaches a certain length, wrap it around your finger or a ring stick.

■ End at edge opposite stopper bead.

Be sure to end on edge opposite stopper bead. Also, since you'll be joining this edge with Rows 1 and 2, end with the row where you string a bugle bead and pass through seed beads.

2 | **Join edges of ring and finish off thread.**

Now you will join the beginning and end of the band you just made. Pass through protruding and recessed bugle beads in alternation. Since the band doesn't have the same number of stitches at beginning and end, make sure the side with the stopper bead on it lines up with side of joined edge.

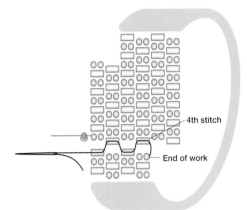
4th stitch

End of work

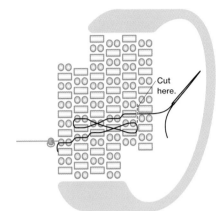
Cut here.

❶ Hold the woven piece edge to edge, aligning the sides where the stopper bead is located. Join edges by passing through recessed and protruding bugle beads in alternation.

❷ Finish off thread: pass through beads near beginning of work, proceeding diagonally, and turning to form intersections 2-3 times. Cut excess thread at edge of a bead. Remove stopper bead at beginning of work. Pass needle through beads near end of work as you did at beginning. Cut thread at the edge of a bead.

TIPS

▦ Keep thread taut when you join edges.

Your work will be made easier if you wrap the ring around your finger as you join the edges. When you pass through beads at beginning and end of work, it's important to pull the thread to keep it taut.

❶ Wrap ring around your index finger from back to front, and hold it in place with your middle finger.

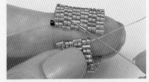

❷ First pass through bugle bead in 4th stitch of Row 1 at beginning of work.

❸ Pull thread each time you pass through a bead to keep tension taut.

▦ Work in different directions when you finish off thread.

After you've joined the edges of the ring, finish off thread, working toward beginning of piece. With thread at beginning of piece, work toward end of piece after removing stopper bead. Remember to pass through two seed beads at a time.

▦ Two-drop variations

You can use other combinations of beads for this stitch. Just be sure to choose beads that will add up to the same length in each stitch (as a bugle bead and two seed beads did for the ring). If you use beads of the same size, they'll line up beautifully when you weave them.

Left: 2 2-mm seed beads and 2 3-mm seed beads
Right: 2 sets of 2-mm seed beads

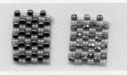

Left: 2 2-mm seed beads and 1 3-mm round bead
Right: 2 2-mm seed beads and 1 3-mm fire-polished bead

✳ BASIC TECHNIQUES ✳

Below we describe basic techniques common to all beading stitches,
such as the preparation and handling of thread.
Mastering these important techniques will make your work easier.

▓ Cutting the thread

Thread length differs with each project, but in general, you'll be working with 1.5-2 meters of thread. The way you hold the scissors is key here: they should be perpendicular to the thread. (If you cut on an angle, the thread ends may fray.)

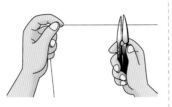

▓ Cutting the thread

Since nylon thread is coated with wax, the end may disappear into the spool if you cut it right at the edge. We suggest cutting it about 2cm away from the spool.

▓ Smoothing the thread

When you unwind beading thread from a spool, you'll find that it comes off in coils. It would be very difficult to work with that way, so be sure to stretch it. Once you've cut the length you need, grasp a length about the wide of your shoulders and pull on it from both ends; repeat.

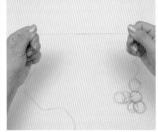

▓ Shifting position of needle

In general, position your needle one-third of the way from the thread end (0.5m from the end if you're working with a 1.5-m length of thread). Thread will, of course, get shorter as you weave. Shift position of needle as you work, sliding it along thread, to avoid fraying or breaking of thread.

▓ Working with a long thread

When you have a long thread you won't be using right away (one that's set aside at the beginning of your work, for instance), wind it around a sticky note to keep it from getting in the way. If you attach the end to the sticky part, it will stay put. Then wind the rest of the thread around the note.

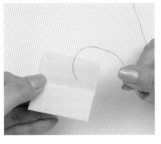
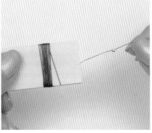

▓ Useful terminology

String (or add) a bead: Pass the needle through a bead for the first time.

Pass through a bead: Pass the needle through a bead that has already been strung.

▓ Passing through beads from work surface

To pass through small beads (11/0 and 8/0 seed beads, for instance), use the point of your needle to position the bead properly, then pass the needle through the hole. With this method, you can string several beads in succession.

▓ Passing through beads

Since you will be passing the needle through the same beads many times, be careful not to sew through other working threads (threads running through the same bead) when you pick beads up.

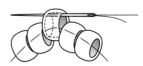

Lesson * 3

Learn tubular peyote stitch.

Now you'll be making jewelry using the tubular peyote stitch. As its name implies, this stitch forms a tube; it is worked in the round in one direction, not back and forth like flat peyote stitch. When the number of stitches in a row (a round) is odd, the tube twists, forming a spiral. With an even number of stitches, the result is a straight tube.

Chiaroscuro Bracelet

Design: Keiko Seki

This bracelet consists mostly of an almost weightless, supple tube woven in tubular peyote stitch.
Since there is an even number of stitches in the first round, the beads in that round join with those in the next round to form a spiral. Select four colors that will blend beautifully into one another.

Bead Ball Necklace

Design: Junko Ando

This gorgeous necklace features bead balls woven in tubular peyote stitch. They are worked with an even number of stitches, so you would expect a vertically straight tube. But we have designed the bead balls so that the larger beads added midway cause them to form spheres. This necklace has impact on the basis of structure alone, so we decided to use earth tones for an ethereal effect.

Chiaroscuro Bracelet

1cm W x 18.5cm L (Peyote stitch: 15cm)

■ Supplies

4.5m beading thread
180 3-mm (8/0) seed beads (gold)
90 3-mm (8/0) seed beads (matte amethyst)
90 3-mm (8/0) seed beads (pearl amethyst)
104 3-mm (8/0) seed beads (metallic purple)
2 3-mm round fire-polished beads (gold)
2 bead caps (antique gold)
Bar-and-ring toggle closure (antique gold)

---

1   Weave a tube in peyote stitch.

❶ Cut thread in half. Leaving a 30-cm end, string 9 seed beads on thread, referring to drawings. Pass through all beads, working in same direction. You have completed Rounds 1 and 2 (Fig. 1).

❷ Pull thread to form a circle, then tie two square knots where indicated in drawing. Pass through first gold seed bead strung (Fig. 2).

❸ Begin Round 3 by stringing a gold seed bead. Then string a bead of the same color as the bead you pass through next. Repeat until you have 9 stitches (Figs. 3 and 4).

❹ Begin Round 4 by passing through a gold seed bead. Continue, stringing a bead of the same color as the one you pass through next, as in Round 3. Repeat these 2 rounds until bracelet is long enough to fit around your wrist. After 100 rounds, tube should be about 15cm long (Figs. 5 and 6).

TIP

■ You don't need to count rounds.

When you're weaving a tube, there's no need to count rounds. All you need to do is weave in peyote stitch, stringing a bead of the same color as the one you just picked up. Since you're working with an odd number of stitches, the tube will form a spiral as it grows. Just make sure that beads are all the same color diagonally.

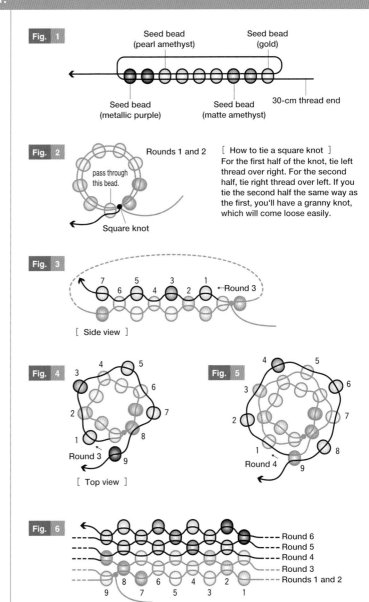

Fig. 1   Seed bead (pearl amethyst)   Seed bead (gold)   Seed bead (metallic purple)   Seed bead (matte amethyst)   30-cm thread end

Fig. 2   Rounds 1 and 2   pass through this bead.   Square knot

[How to tie a square knot]
For the first half of the knot, tie left thread over right. For the second half, tie right thread over left. If you tie the second half the same way as the first, you'll have a granny knot, which will come loose easily.

Fig. 3   ←Round 3   [Side view]

Fig. 4   Round 3   [Top view]

Fig. 5   Round 4

Fig. 6   Round 6   Round 5   Round 4   Round 3   Rounds 1 and 2

■ Joining new thread

You need 4.5m thread to make this bracelet. But since it's very awkward to work with thread that long, you'll be working with thread half that length. When there is only 20cm of thread remaining on your needle, it's time to join new thread (Figs. 7 and 8).

❶ Set old thread aside, and string a stopper bead on new thread 5cm from the end.

❷ Run needle with new thread on it through beads in bracelet in a zigzag pattern. Make two half-hitch knots as you go along (Fig. 8).

❸ After you've woven 3cm with new thread, thread a needle with the old thread and finish it off in the same way.

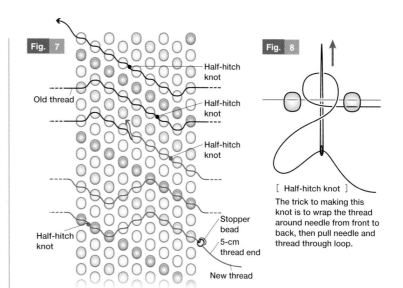

Fig. 7

Half-hitch knot

Old thread

Half-hitch knot

Half-hitch knot

Half-hitch knot

Stopper bead

5-cm thread end

New thread

Fig. 8

[Half-hitch knot]
The trick to making this knot is to wrap the thread around needle from front to back, then pull needle and thread through loop.

---

2   Attach closure to ends of tube and finish off thread.

❶ Using thread at end of tube, pass through every other bead 4 times; repeat. Pull thread (Fig. 9).

❷ String bead cap, metallic purple seed beads, a fire-polished bead, and ring half of closure to form a loop. Pass needle through beads in loop again, then back into tube (Fig. 10).

❸ Finish off thread. Just as you do when you add new thread, run needle through beads diagonally, making half-hitch knots as you go. Cut excess thread at edge of a bead (Fig. 11).

❹ Thread needle with thread at beginning of work, and attach bar half of closure, following directions in Step ② (Fig. 12).

❺ Pass needle back to beads in tube; finish off thread as in Step ③.

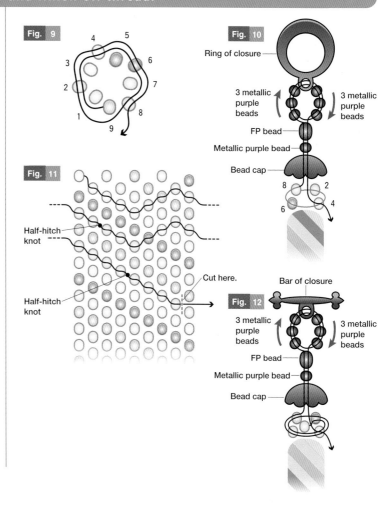

Fig. 9

Fig. 10

Ring of closure

3 metallic purple beads

3 metallic purple beads

FP bead

Metallic purple bead

Bead cap

Fig. 11

Half-hitch knot

Half-hitch knot

Cut here.

Fig. 12

Bar of closure

3 metallic purple beads

3 metallic purple beads

FP bead

Metallic purple bead

Bead cap

Beaded Bead Necklace

46cm L (Bead balls: 1.5cm diameter)

■Supplies

6.9m beading thread

304 2-mm (11/0) seed beads (pale pink)

84 2.5-mm triangle beads (pink)

84 3-mm (8/0) seed beads (pale pink)

108 3-mm round pressed-glass beads (pale green)

54 2 x 3-mm button fire-polished beads (brown)

84 4-mm round fire-polished beads (pearl pink)

7 10-mm round fire-polished beads (translucent or pastel color) ※

20 4-mm bicone crystal beads (light brown)

Bar-and-ring toggle closure (antique gold)

※These beads are enclosed in the bead balls.

---

1   Weave a peyote-stitch tube and make Beaded Bead.

❶ Cut 80cm thread. Round 1: leaving a 20-cm end, string 6 seed beads. Pass through all beads once again (Fig. 1).

❷ Pull thread to form a circle, then tie a square knot. Pass through first seed bead strung again (Fig. 2).

❸ Round 2: string 2-mm seed beads, one at a time, between beads in Round 1; you should have 12 stitches. Pass through first 2-mm seed bead in Round 2 again and step up to Round 3 (Fig. 3).

❹ From Round 3 to Round 9, continue weaving tube as in Step ③, changing beads each row (Figs. 4-6).

ⓉⒾⓅⓈ

■ Don't forget to step up at the end of each round.

There is an even number of stitches in Round 1 of this tube. Therefore, you end a round by joining the first and last bead strung. The important thing to remember is to "step up" at the end of each round, meaning pass through the first bead strung on that round, then begin the next round.

■ Keep thread taut as you work.

Since you're using larger beads at the center of the tube, it will be wider at that point. If your thread tension is loose, you'll have a hard time stabilizing the bead that goes inside the tube. So take the time to pull the thread taut as often as possible.

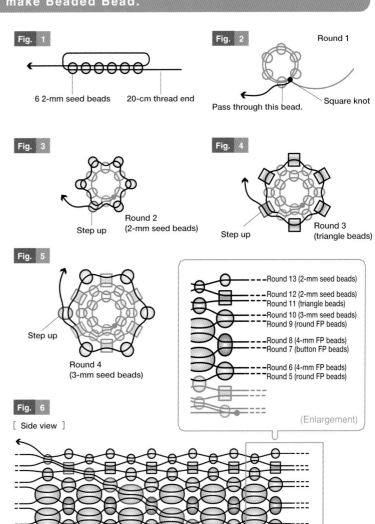

Fig. 1
6 2-mm seed beads   20-cm thread end

Fig. 2   Round 1
Pass through this bead.   Square knot

Fig. 3
Step up
Round 2 (2-mm seed beads)

Fig. 4
Step up
Round 3 (triangle beads)

Fig. 5
Step up
Round 4 (3-mm seed beads)

Round 13 (2-mm seed beads)
Round 12 (2-mm seed beads)
Round 11 (triangle beads)
Round 10 (3-mm seed beads)
Round 9 (round FP beads)
Round 8 (4-mm FP beads)
Round 7 (button FP beads)
Round 6 (4-mm FP beads)
Round 5 (round FP beads)
(Enlargement)

Fig. 6
[Side view]

For step up for each round, see beads outlined in blue.

❺ When you've finished Round 9 (round fire-polished beads), insert 10-mm fire-polished bead into tube, with hole at top. Weave remaining rounds (Figs. 6 and 7).

❻ Pass through the 6 2-mm seed beads in Round 13 and pull thread (Fig. 8).

❼ Pass needle back through beads in tube, turning to form intersections and making half-hitch knots as you go along. Cut excess thread at edge of a bead. Finish off thread at beginning of work in same way.

❽ Make a total of 7 bead balls, following directions in Steps ①-⑦.

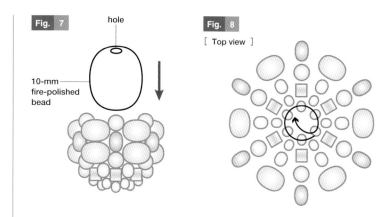

Fig. 7

hole

10-mm fire-polished bead

Fig. 8

[Top view]

2 Join bead balls and make necklace.

❶ Cut 130-cm length of thread and string beads on center of thread, referring to drawing (Fig. 9).

❷ String 4 2-mm seed beads, ring of closure and 4 more 2-mm seed beads, forming a loop. Pass needle through beads in loop again, then through beads strung in Step ① until you reach center of necklace. Set thread aside (Fig. 10).

❸ Attach bar of closure to other end of necklace, following directions in Step ②. Pass needle through beads strung in Step ① until you reach center of necklace. Join thread to thread set aside in Step ② with a square knot (Fig. 11).

❹ Run needle back through beads and cut thread at edge of a bead. Repeat with other thread end.

TIP

■ **Double-check position of bead inside bead ball.**

When you assemble the necklace, you'll be passing the needle through the hole in the 10-mm beads inside the bead balls. Make sure the hole in each 10-mm bead is at the top of the bead ball. If a bead shifts, reposition it with an awl or similar tool.

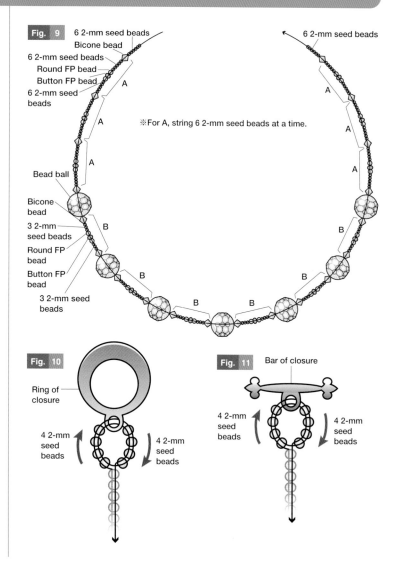

Fig. 9

6 2-mm seed beads
Bicone bead
6 2-mm seed beads
Round FP bead
Button FP bead
6 2-mm seed beads

6 2-mm seed beads

A

A

A

A

A

A

A

※For A, string 6 2-mm seed beads at a time.

Bead ball

Bicone bead

3 2-mm seed beads

Round FP bead

Button FP bead

3 2-mm seed beads

B

B

B

B

B

B

Fig. 10

Ring of closure

4 2-mm seed beads

4 2-mm seed beads

Fig. 11

Bar of closure

4 2-mm seed beads

4 2-mm seed beads

Seagreen
Necklace

Design: Yumi Kizaki

Rich, gleaming shades of green and a gorgeous
spiral combine to make this enchanting necklace.
It is made with an even number of stitches, but the
spiral is created by shifting the positions of the
beads a little in each round. The use of different-
sized beads, as well as different colors, adds
interest to the spiral.

Seagreen Necklace

Finished measurements:

1-1.5-cm W x 48cm L (Peyote stitch: 45cm)

Supplies

12.5m beading thread

802 3-mm (8/0) seed beads (pale green)

402 2-mm (11/0) seed beads (dark green)

400 2-mm (11/0) seed beads (emerald green)

400 2-mm (11/0) seed beads (silver)

29 2-mm (11/0) seed beads (pale green)

400 3-mm (8/0) round fire-polished beads (emerald green)

Bar-and-ring toggle closure (silver)

❶ Cut a manageable length of thread. String 12 beads, referring to drawing and leaving a 50-cm end. Pass through all beads again, moving in same direction, to close circle. Tie a square knot. You have just completed Rounds 1 and 2. Pass through first 2 silver seed beads strung, and step up to Round 3 (Fig. 1).

❷ Begin Round 3 by stringing a silver 2-mm seed bead. Work 12 stitches, stringing a bead of the same color as the one you just picked up. Pass through first silver seed bead strung and step up to Round 4 (Fig. 2).

❸ Continue weaving in the same way until necklace is desired length. When only 20cm thread remains on needle, add new thread (see p. 17). The piece should measure 45cm after 400 rounds (Figs. 3 and 4).

> **TIP**
>
> ## ■ Weaving a spiral
>
> Since the rounds of the tube have an even number of stitches, you'll be stepping up from round to round (passing through the first silver seed bead in round). If you add a bead of the same type as the one you just picked up, the tube should form a spiral after you step up.

❹ Attach ring of closure. Pass needle through beads in last round woven. Add more beads and ring of closure, referring to drawing. Pass needle back through beads in tube and finish off thread (Fig. 5).

❺ Using thread at beginning of work, pass through beads in Round 1 of tube. Add more beads and bar of closure, referring to drawing. Pass needle back through beads in tube and finish off thread (Fig. 6).

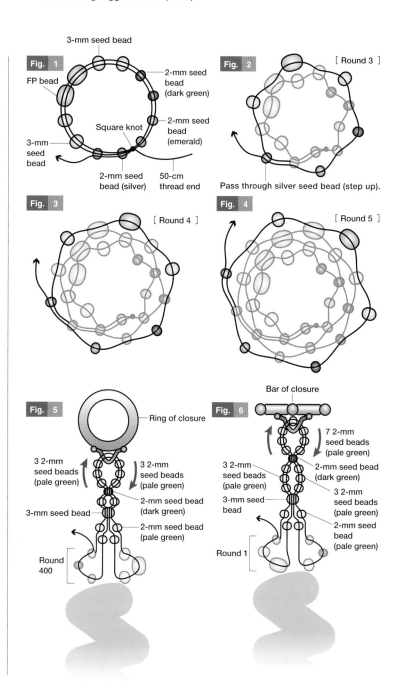

Fig. 1
3-mm seed bead
FP bead
2-mm seed bead (dark green)
Square knot
2-mm seed bead (emerald)
3-mm seed bead
2-mm seed bead (silver)
50-cm thread end

Fig. 2
[Round 3]
Pass through silver seed bead (step up).

Fig. 3
[Round 4]

Fig. 4
[Round 5]

Fig. 5
Ring of closure
3 2-mm seed beads (pale green)
3 2-mm seed beads (pale green)
2-mm seed bead (dark green)
3-mm seed bead
2-mm seed bead (pale green)
Round 400

Fig. 6
Bar of closure
7 2-mm seed beads (pale green)
3 2-mm seed beads (pale green)
2-mm seed bead (dark green)
3 2-mm seed beads (pale green)
3-mm seed bead
2-mm seed bead (pale green)
Round 1

Lesson * 4

Learn three-dimensional peyote stitch.

Now you'll be learning how to weave a three-dimensional piece in peyote stitch. You start out by weaving the bottom. Then you make increases between the diagonal lines to form the sides. When you weave the sides, you'll be working in one direction, stepping up each round.

Miniature Toto Bag in Vitamin Colors

Design: Junko Ando

This tiny tote bag is not much more than 2cm high, but the vivid color scheme, reminiscent of citrus fruits, is amazingly energizing. You can even use it as a charm: just slip a length of ball chain under the handles.

Miniature
Jewelry Box

Design: Kimie Suto

The flowers woven into the sides of this
lovely little jewelry box and its pastel colors
are likely to bring on an attack of nostalgia.
You'll find it's a great place to keep your
rings and other precious items. The four
sides of the box are identical, but pay close
attention to the drawings while you work so
you position the beads correctly. The
bottom of the box and the lid are made in
the same way at the beginning.

Miniature Tote Bag in Vitamin Colors

■Finished measurements:

3.5cm W x 2cm H (minus handles)

■Supplies

3m beading thread
408 1.6-mm cylinder beads (ivory)
216 1.6-mm cylinder beads (yellow)
160 1.6-mm cylinder beads (green)
110 1.6-mm cylinder beads (orange)
16cm ball chain (gold)
2 clam-shell bead tips (gold)
Lobster closure and chain tab (gold)

1 Weave a peyote-stitch square for bottom of bag.

❶ Cut 2m thread. Leaving a 20-cm end, string 4 each yellow and orange beads in alternation. Pass needle through all beads again, moving in same direction, to close circle. You have just woven Rounds 1 and 2. Pass through first yellow bead strung again (Fig. 1).

❷ In Round 3, string a yellow bead, an orange bead, and another yellow bead (increase made). Skip orange bead in previous round and pass through a yellow bead (Fig. 2).

❸ Continue stringing 3 beads to make increases, referring to drawing. Pass through first orange bead strung in this round and step up to next round (Fig. 3).

❹ Make increases in Round 4 by stringing 3 beads, only at corners, adding a green bead between beads in previous round, referring to drawing. Pass through first yellow bead strung in this round and step up to next round (Fig. 4).

❺ Make increases in Round 5 by stringing 3 beads, only at corners, adding an ivory bead between beads in previous round (Fig. 5).

❻ Continue in the same way, adding green beads between beads in previous round in Round 6, ivory beads in Round 7, and green and ivory beads in Round 8, referring to drawing (Fig. 6).

❼ After completing Round 8, pass through first yellow bead strung in round and step up. Now you will be weaving one of the sides, but before you begin, finish off thread at beginning of work. Pass needle through beads on the diagonal, turning to form intersections 2-3 times. Cut excess thread at edge of a bead.

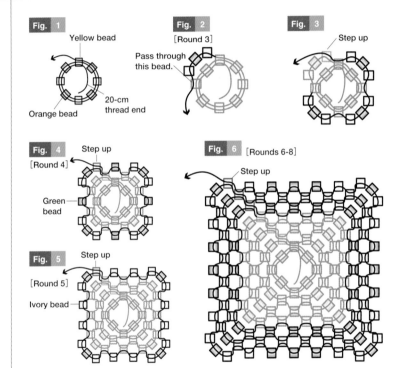

Fig. 1
Yellow bead
Orange bead
20-cm thread end

Fig. 2
[Round 3]
Pass through this bead.

Fig. 3
Step up

Fig. 4
[Round 4]
Step up
Green bead

Fig. 5
[Round 5]
Step up
Ivory bead

Fig. 6
[Rounds 6-8]
Step up

ⓉⒾⓅⓈ

■ Make increases next to the orange beads.

The orange lines that extend outward diagonally from the center will become diagonals that cut through the square (the bottom). The key to weaving the bottom is stringing one yellow bead at a time at each side of the orange beads, and making increases evenly. Between the diagonals, pass through beads in the previous round while adding one bead at a time, to form a square. The number of beads between the diagonal lines will increase by one each round, but you'll still be passing through the first bead in each round (outlined in blue in the drawings) to step up to the next round.

■ Bottom: aim for a rippled surface

The bottom of the bag is woven into a square shape, but as you proceed, you'll notice that its surface isn't flat, but rippled. The orange beads make the bag look like it has feet.

2 Weave sides of bag in peyote stitch, in the round.

❶ Weave sides, using thread extending from bottom of bag. You won't be making increases for the sides, just adding cylinder beads between beads in previous round, moving in a specific direction. For Round 1, you'll be adding orange beads on the diagonals, and ivory beads between diagonals (Fig. 7).

❷ At end of Round 1, pass through first orange bead strung and step up to Round 2 (Fig. 8).

❸ Starting with Round 2, weave 23 rounds of peyote stitch, referring to drawing for color placement (Fig. 9).

❹ Finish off thread: pass needle back through beads, diagonally, turning 2-3 times to form intersections.

TIP

■ Always be aware of the beginning of a round.

At the end of a round, you will be passing through the first bead strung in that round and stepping up to the next round. Each round will begin one stitch away from the previous round, in the direction in which you're working. In Fig. 9, the beads outlined in blue indicate the beginning of each round.

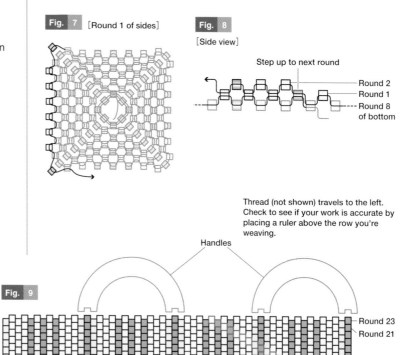

Fig. 7 [Round 1 of sides]

Fig. 8 [Side view]

Step up to next round
Round 2
Round 1
Round 8 of bottom

Thread (not shown) travels to the left. Check to see if your work is accurate by placing a ruler above the row you're weaving.

Handles

Fig. 9

Round 23
Round 21
Round 11
Round 1
Starting point for sides

3 Make handles and attach to sides; add findings.

❶ Cut a 50-cm length of thread. String a stopper bead on it, leaving a 20-cm end. Pass through beads on top of bag where handle is to be attached, referring to drawing. String yellow beads for handle (Fig. 10).

❷ Beginning with Row 2, add an orange bead at center. Weave 35 rows, forming intersections as indicated in drawing (Fig. 11).

❸ At end of Row 35, align handle with top of bag, referring to drawings, and join the two edges. Run needle back through beads and finish off thread. Remove stopper bead from beginning of work and finish off thread. Make other handle in the same way and join to top of bag (Fig. 12).

❹ Attach chain. Attach a bead tip at each end of chain. Join bead tip and closure with a jump ring (Fig. 13).

❺ Slide chain under handles.

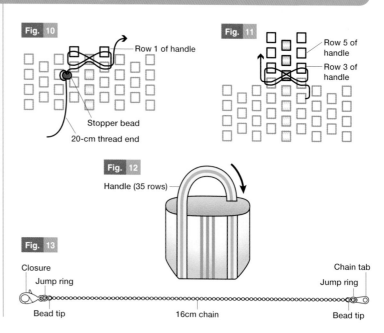

Fig. 10
Row 1 of handle
Stopper bead
20-cm thread end

Fig. 11
Row 5 of handle
Row 3 of handle

Fig. 12
Handle (35 rows)

Fig. 13
Closure
Jump ring
Bead tip
16cm chain
Chain tab
Jump ring
Bead tip

Miniature Jewelry Box

■Supplies

5m beading thread
864 1.6-mm cylinder beads (pink)
327 1.6-mm cylinder beads (purple)
232 1.6-mm cylinder beads (green)
10-mm designer flower bead (purple)
4-mm round glass pearl bead (white)

■Finished measurements:

2.3cm W x 2.3cm D x 2.8cm H (box only)

1 Weave bottom and sides of box.

❶ Cut 2m thread. Leaving a 20-cm end, string 8 purple cylinder beads, then tie a square knot. You have completed Rounds 1 and 2 of the bottom of the box. Pass through first bead strung again (Fig. 1).

❷ In Round 3, work peyote stitch, stringing 3 purple beads at a time for increases. Pass through first purple bead strung in this round, and step up to next round (Fig. 2).

❸ In Round 4, make increases (by stringing 2 beads) only at corners, adding a pink cylinder bead between beads in previous round, referring to drawing. Pass through first purple bead strung in this round and step up to next round (Fig. 2).

❹ In Rounds 5-12, add cylinder beads as indicated in drawing to form square bottom (Fig. 3).

❺ Begin weaving sides of box. You won't be making increases for the sides; simply weave 4 repetitions of pattern shown in drawing for each round until you have 30 rounds. Always be aware of starting point (bead outlined in blue in Fig. 4) as you weave. When there is only 20cm thread remaining, join 2m new thread (Fig. 4).

❻ Finish off thread at end of work by passing needle through beads on the diagonal, turning 2-3 times to form intersections. Finish off thread at beginning of work in same way.

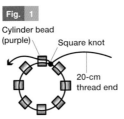

Fig. 1
Cylinder bead (purple)   Square knot
20-cm thread end

Fig. 2
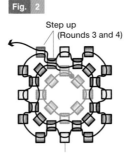
Step up (Rounds 3 and 4)
Cylinder bead (pink)

Fig. 3   Rounds 5-12 (bottom of box)
Sides begin here.

Fig. 4
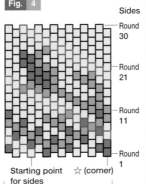
Sides
Round 30
Round 21
Round 11
Round 1
Starting point for sides   ☆ (corner)
1 side of box
Repeat pattern 4 times.←
※In Round 1 of sides, don't pass through corner beads (★ in Fig. 3); instead add 1 purple bead at a time (☆ in Fig. 4).

TIPS

■ Use purple beads for increases; add pink beads between diagonals.

On the diagonals, all increases are made with purple beads. All cylinder beads strung between diagonals are pink.

■ Number of increases is different in each round.

Remember that the number of increases is not the same in every round. When you start a new round, be sure to consult Fig. 3. Refer to the following list for the number of beads in each round.

Rounds 3, 8: 3 beads at a time
Rounds 4, 5, 9, 10: 2 beads at a time
Rounds 6, 11: 1 bead
Rounds 7, 12: 0 beads

2 Weave lid in peyote stitch.

❶ Cut a 1.5-m length of thread. String 8 pink cylinder beads, leaving a 30-cm end, and tie a square knot as you did on bottom. Pass through first pink bead strung, and weave a square in peyote stitch, adding cylinder beads as indicated in drawing (17 rounds). You will be following the same steps in Rounds 3-12 as you did on bottom of box (Fig. 5).

🅣🅘🅟

▮ String beads of the same color in the same row.

The color of the cylinder beads will change every round, but you'll be adding beads of the same color in each round. Check to make sure you're adding the right color before you begin the next round. Refer to the following list.

Pink: Rounds 1, 2, 3, 6, 7, 12, 13, 14
Green: Rounds 4, 5, 8, 9
Purple: Rounds 10, 11, 15, 16, 17

❷ Finish off thread at end of work by passing needle through beads on the diagonal and forming intersections 2-3 times.

❸ Use thread at beginning of work to make decoration for lid. String flower bead, pearl bead and a purple cylinder bead; pass needle back through pearl and flower beads. Pass needle through beads in lid, then finish off thread (Fig. 6).

Fig. 5 Lid (17 rounds)

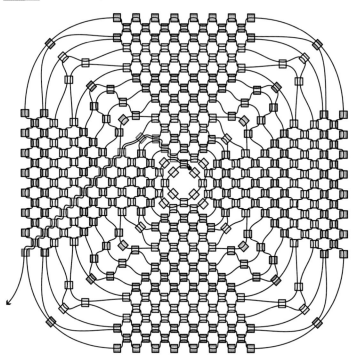

Fig. 6

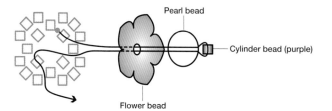

Pearl bead

Cylinder bead (purple)

Flower bead

Lesson * 5

Learn circular peyote stitch.

Now we're going to show you how to work circular peyote stitch. To make a flat circular piece, you work from the center out, making increases. The beads form a circular, rippled pattern like a frill, a vibrant piece with a lot of movement. You can also enclose a cabochon or a button in circular peyote stitch.

Four-Color Round Appliqué and Covered Button

Design: Hiroe Takagi

The button on the strap on the cellular phone case in the photo is covered with circular peyote stitch. At the other end of the strap is a flat peyote-stitch round appliqué. These ornaments make beautiful accents for jackets, coats or blouses. Make an original piece by using different types of beads, adding beads, or designing your own pattern.

Curly Bracelet

Design: Yumiko Watanabe

A series of open coils forms this unique
bracelet. This design fits the wrist perfectly,
light as air on your wrist. The beginning is
worked in flat, not circular, peyote stitch.
The coils form later when you begin making
increases. We chose silver beads for an
elegant, feminine look.

Four-Color Round Appliqué and Covered Button

17mm diameter (circle); 22mm diameter (covered button)

■Supplies

[Appliqué]
0.7m beading thread
18 1.6-mm cylinder beads (pale blue)
18 1.6-mm cylinder beads (blue)
24 1.6-mm cylinder beads (brown)
24 1.6-mm cylinder beads (yellow)
3-mm round bead (bronze)

[Covered button]
1m beading thread
48 1.6-mm cylinder beads (pale blue)
42 1.6-mm cylinder beads (blue)
30 1.6-mm cylinder beads (brown)
36 1.6-mm cylinder beads (yellow)
6 3-mm (8/0) seed beads (silver)
18 1.5-mm (15/0) seed beads (silver)
3-mm round bead (bronze)
15-mm (diameter) shank button (blue)

1 Weave a peyote-stitch circle.

❶ Round 1: string 6 pale-blue cylinder beads on thread, leaving a 25-cm end. Tie a square knot. Pass through first bead strung (Fig. 1).

❷ Round 2 (Beads 7-12): add a blue cylinder bead between pale-blue beads. Pass through first blue bead strung again (Fig. 2).

❸ Round 3 (Beads 13-24): make increases by adding 2 brown cylinder beads between the blue beads. At end of round, pass through first brown bead strung again (Fig. 3).

❹ Round 4 (Beads 25-36): Add one pale-blue or blue bead, in alternation, between brown beads. At end of round pass through first pale-blue bead strung in round again (Fig. 4).

❺ Round 5 (Beads 37-48): make increases, adding a yellow cylinder bead between the pale-blue and blue beads. At end of round pass through first yellow bead strung again (Fig. 5).

❻ Round 6 (Beads 48-66): make increases, adding two brown beads or one pale-blue bead, in alternation, between yellow beads. At end of round pass through first brown bead strung in round again (Fig. 6).

TIPS

■ **Remember to step up to each new row.**

At the end of each round, be sure to step up to the next one by passing through the first bead added on that round (pass through bead outlined in red in Figs. 2-6).

■ **Make increases when you add brown beads.**

In Round 3, you'll be adding 2 brown beads at a time between beads in previous row. In Round 6, you'll be adding 2 brown beads and one pale-blue bead in alternation. Beads in all other colors are added one at a time.

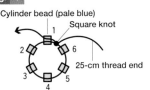

Fig. 1
Cylinder bead (pale blue) Square knot
25-cm thread end

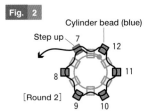

Fig. 2
Cylinder bead (blue)
Step up
[Round 2]

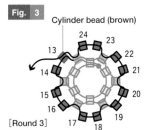

Fig. 3
Cylinder bead (brown)
[Round 3]

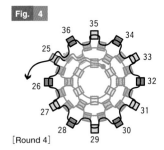

Fig. 4
[Round 4]

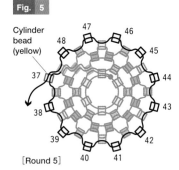

Fig. 5
Cylinder bead (yellow)
[Round 5]

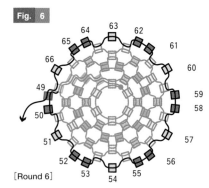

Fig. 6
[Round 6]

7 Round 7 (last round: Beads 67-84): string a blue bead, a yellow bead, and another yellow bead; repeat. At end of round, pass through first brown bead strung on Round 6 (Fig. 7).

8 Finish off thread at end of work by running needle through beads, diagonally, forming intersections along the way (Fig. 8).

9 String round bronze bead on thread at beginning of work. Pass through beads in Round 1, referring to drawing (Fig. 9).

10 Finish off thread, running needle through beads on the diagonal and forming intersections. Appliqué to fabric or garment.

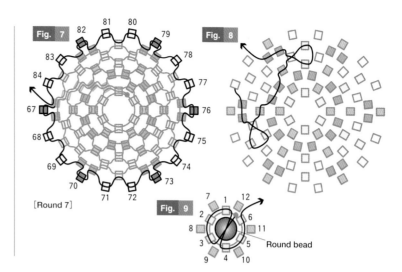

[Round 7]

Fig. 7 · Fig. 8 · Fig. 9 · Round bead

---

2 | **Cover a button with circular peyote stitch.**

1 Follow directions for four-color circle up to and including Round 7.

2 Beginning with Round 8, place woven piece on top of button and weave so as to enclose it. Add beads between beads in previous row, following directions below. Pass through first bead in each row (outlined in red in drawing) and step up to next round (Fig. 10).

Round 8 (Beads 85-102): pale blue, brown, pale blue (one at a time); repeat

Round 9 (Beads 103-120): yellow, yellow, blue (one at a time); repeat

Round 10 (Beads 121-138): pale blue

Round 11 (Beads 139-156): blue

Round 12 (Beads 157-174): 1.5-mm seed beads

3 Run thread through beads until you reach Round 9. Add a 3-mm seed bead between adjacent yellow beads in Round 9. Finish off thread at end of round (Fig. 11).

4 String a round bead on thread at beginning of work. Pass through beads in Round 1 and finish off thread (Fig. 11).

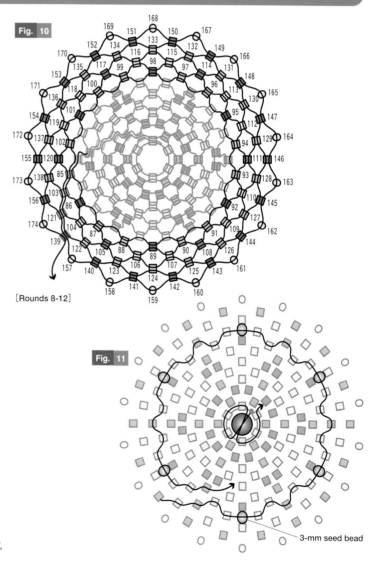

Fig. 10

[Rounds 8-12]

Fig. 11 · 3-mm seed bead

Curly Bracelet

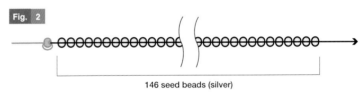

■Supplies

2.5m beading thread
294 2-mm (11/0) seed beads (silver)
328 2-mm (11/0) seed beads (light bronze)
17-mm (diameter) flower button (silver)

■Finished measurements:

1.3cm x 18cm (Peyote stitch: 16cm)

1 Weave 4 rows of peyote stitch, making increases as you go along.

❶ String a stopper bead on thread, leaving a 20-cm end. Use a clip or similar device to hold stopper bead in place (Fig. 1).

❷ String 146 seed beads to form Rows 1 and 2 (Fig. 2).

❸ In Row 3, string 2 silver beads at a time to make increases. Curves should start to form in the piece (Fig. 3).

❹ In Row 4, add one light-bronze seed bead at a time. As you rotate the piece while weaving, the bracelet should be forming a beautiful spiral (Fig. 4).

ⓉⒾⓅⓈ

■ Use a clip to keep tension taut.

Since you will be stringing a lot of beads for Rows 1 and 2, the stopper bead alone can't keep the tension from loosening. The curves in the bracelet won't look right unless tension is tight, so use a clip or similar device to hold stopper bead firmly in place. Make sure it grips the thread properly. We recommend bulldog clips, which you can find at office-supply stores.

■ In Row 4, rotate piece as you weave.

In Row 4, rotate the woven piece, always in the same direction, so that the curves in Row 3 form a spiral.

Fig. 1

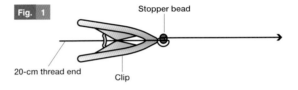

Stopper bead

20-cm thread end

Clip

Fig. 2

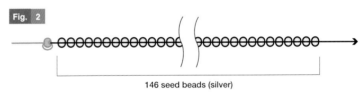

146 seed beads (silver)

Fig. 3 [Row 3] (increase row)

Fig. 4 [Row 4]

Seed beads (light bronze)

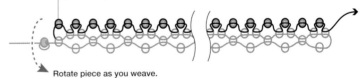

Rotate piece as you weave.

2 Attach closure and weave Row 5.

❶ String a light-bronze bead on same thread, and pass through last light-bronze bead in Row 4. Add 5 seed beads and button (closure), forming a loop, as shown in drawing. Pass needle through same beads again for added strength (Fig. 5).

❷ Weave Row 5, adding one light-bronze bead at a time. After you've strung the last bead and picked up a bead from previous row, remove clip and stopper bead, and tie a square knot (Fig. 6).

❸ With thread from end of work, pass through beads at left edge of Rows 4 and 5. Add 3 light-bronze beads, 2 silver beads and about 25 more light-bronze beads (just enough to accommodate button half of closure).
Pass through 2 silver beads, then string 3 light-bronze beads. Pass through seed beads at left edge of Rows 4 and 5. Pass through beads again for added strength. Finish off thread, and thread at beginning of work (Fig. 7).

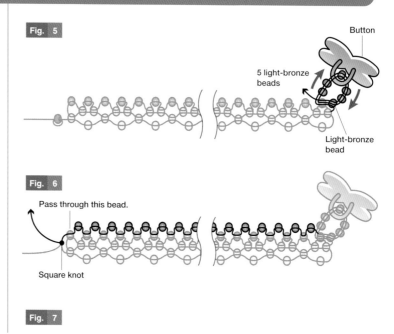

Fig. 5

Button

5 light-bronze beads

Light-bronze bead

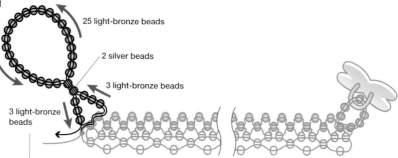

Fig. 6

Pass through this bead.

Square knot

Fig. 7

25 light-bronze beads

2 silver beads

3 light-bronze beads

3 light-bronze beads

Frilled Pendant

Design: Yumiko Watanabe

To make the pendant, we enclosed a cabochon with no holes in a circular peyote stitch frame, creating the frills by increasing the number of stitches in the frame. You could thread chain through the loop attached to the back of the pendant. But we prefer the matching necklace, with its whimsical corncob accents, because it complements the pendant very nicely.

Frilled Pendant

■Finished measurements:

1cm W x 4.5cm diameter (pendant) (Necklace: 50cm L)

■Supplies

5.5m beading thread
258 1.6-mm cylinder beads (bronze)
18 1.5-mm (15/0) seed beads (bronze)
264 2-mm (11/0) seed beads (dark red)
336 2-mm (11/0) seed beads (light red)
523 2-mm (11/0) seed beads (brown aurora)
15-mm cabochon (reddish brown)
Bar-and-ring toggle closure (antique gold)

1 Enclose cabochon in circular peyote stitch; make frame for pendant.

❶ Cut a 1.5-m length of thread. Round 1: string 3 cylinder beads, leaving a 20-cm end.
Pass through beads just strung, moving in same direction. Pass through first bead strung (Fig. 1).

❷ Rounds 2-8: weave in the round, adding cylinder beads as indicated in drawing. In Round 2 (Beads 4-6), Round 4 (Beads 13-18), Round 6 (Beads 31-42) and Round 7 (Beads 43-54), add one bead at a time while passing through beads in previous round. In Round 3 (Beads 7-12) and Round 5 (Beads 19-30), add 2 beads at a time. In Round 8 (Beads 55-72), add 2 beads, then one bead, in alternation for the increase (Fig. 2).

❸ Starting in Round 9, place cabochon in center of circle, and enclose it in beads, adding one cylinder bead at a time. In Round 14 (last round), add one 1.5-mm seed bead at a time (Figs. 3 and 4).

❹ With same thread on it, pass needle back into woven piece, bringing it out at Round 9. Set aside.

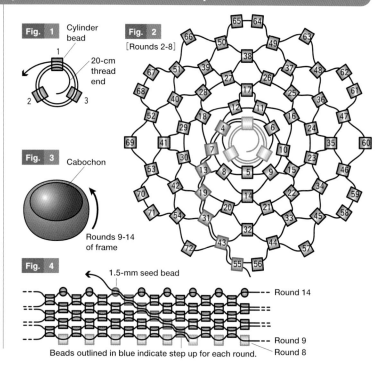

Fig. 1 Cylinder bead
1
20-cm thread end
2   3

Fig. 2 [Rounds 2-8]

Fig. 3 Cabochon
Rounds 9-14 of frame

Fig. 4   1.5-mm seed bead
Round 14
Round 9
Round 8
Beads outlined in blue indicate step up for each round.

2 Attach frill to cabochon frame.

❶ Cut a 2-m length thread. Finish off old thread, passing through beads in frame as you go. Bring needle out from a cylinder bead in Round 11.

❷ Pass through beads in Round 11 of frame and weave 8-round frill. Add 2-mm seed beads between beads in previous rows, as follows (Fig. 5).
Round 1 (increase round): add 2 dark-red beads
Round 2 (increase round): add one dark-red bead and 2 dark-red beads, in alternation
Round 3: add one dark-red bead
Round 4: add one light-red bead
Round 5 (increase row): add one light-red and 2 light-red beads in alternation
Round 6: add one light-red bead
Rounds 7, 8: add one brown aurora bead

❸ Finish off thread.

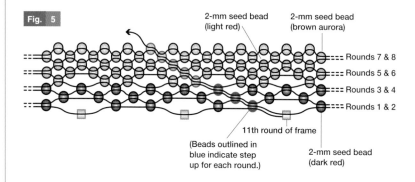

Fig. 5   2-mm seed bead (light red)   2-mm seed bead (brown aurora)
Rounds 7 & 8
Rounds 5 & 6
Rounds 3 & 4
Rounds 1 & 2
11th round of frame
(Beads outlined in blue indicate step up for each round.)
2-mm seed bead (dark red)

3 Attach a loop to back of pendant frame.

❶ Make a loop using thread set aside at end of frame. Pass through beads in Round 9 of frame, adding one cylinder bead at a time. Weave 32 6-stitch rows of flat peyote stitch (Fig. 6).

❷ Pass through beads in Round 6 of frame (wrong side) to join. Finish off thread (Figs. 7 and 8).

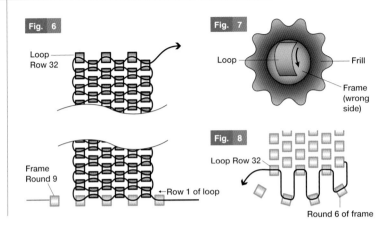

Fig. 6
Loop Row 32

Frame Round 9
← Row 1 of loop

Fig. 7
Loop — — Frill
— Frame (wrong side)

Fig. 8
Loop Row 32
Round 6 of frame

4 Make necklace with corncob motifs.

❶ Cut a 2-m length of thread. String 4 brown aurora 2-mm seed beads (core beads), leaving a 30-cm end. Then add 4 dark-red 2-mm seed beads (kernels), passing through brown aurora beads from underneath. Pull thread gently, sliding dark-red beads to the left (Fig. 9).

❷ Continue in the same way, adding a total of 6 sets of 4 dark-red beads around the core. You have made one corncob (Fig. 10).

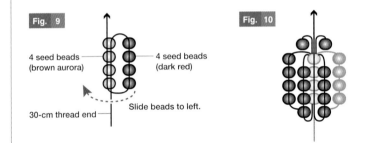

Fig. 9
4 seed beads (brown aurora)   4 seed beads (dark red)
30-cm thread end   Slide beads to left.

Fig. 10

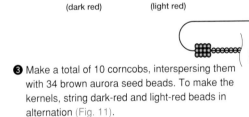

図 11
34 beads (brown aurora)   34 beads (brown aurora)
1st corncob (dark red)   2nd corncob (light red)
10th corncob (light red)

❸ Make a total of 10 corncobs, interspersing them with 34 brown aurora seed beads. To make the kernels, string dark-red and light-red beads in alternation (Fig. 11).

❹ Using same thread, string 8 brown aurora beads and ring of closure to form a loop. Pass through working threads inside corncob, making half-hitch knots as you go along, and pass needle through beads in loop once again. Pass through seed beads underneath corncob and cut thread at edge of a bead (Fig. 12).

❺ String 4 brown aurora beads, bar of closure and 3 more brown aurora beads on thread set aside at beginning of work. Make a loop, following directions in Step ④. Finish off thread (Fig. 13).

❻ Thread necklace through loop on pendant.

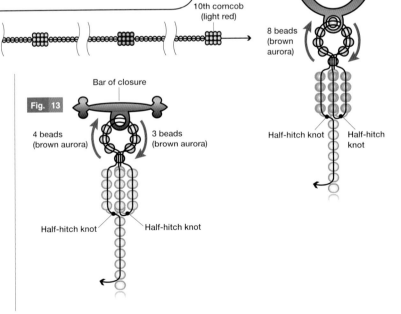

Fig. 12
Ring of closure
8 beads (brown aurora)
Half-hitch knot   Half-hitch knot

Fig. 13
Bar of closure
4 beads (brown aurora)   3 beads (brown aurora)
Half-hitch knot   Half-hitch knot

Lesson * 6

Learn odd-count peyote stitch and how to make increases and decreases.

Our last lesson is in two parts: (1) weaving pieces in odd-count peyote stitch, and (2) learning how to increase and decrease stitches at the edge of a piece. Both these techniques involve making turns. If you make increases or decreases in the middle of a woven piece, it will gather or take on a fan shape. But if you make those same increases and decreases at the edges of a piece, you'll be able to create a wide variety of flat shapes.

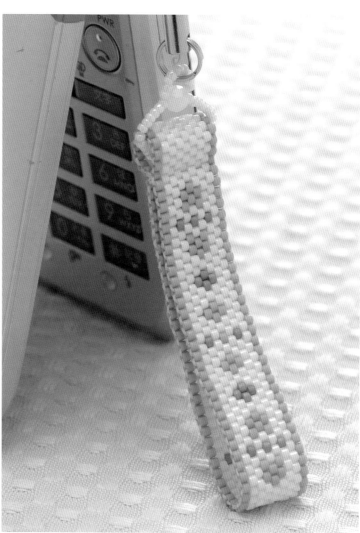

Cell Phone Strap with Floral Pattern

Design: Kajiwara Mio

Tiny flowers are woven into this long, narrow strap worked in flat peyote stitch. The strap is just the right size for a woman. Since you'll be working in odd-count peyote, you'll need to make turns sometimes when proceeding from one row to the next.

Badge Brooch

Design: Mio Kajiwara

This brooch is shaped like a badge, but there the resemblance ends. Translucent beads and fringe give it brilliance, while the simple design gives it a polished look. It will look just as wonderful on a hat or handbag as on a blouse or jacket. You begin working in odd-count peyote and decrease toward the end, so the bottom comes to a point.

Flower Garden Choker

Design: Miwako Shimizu

Save this dazzling choker, with its lacy flower
motifs, for the most festive occasions.
We used only one color for an opulent look. The
five petals in each flower motif are worked in flat
peyote stitch; decreases shape the petals.
The flowers are connected by seed beads.
For accents we added drop beads and leaf-
shaped loops.

Cell Phone Strap with Floral Pattern

■Finished measurements:

1.2cm W x 27cm L (Peyote stitch: 12cm L)

■Supplies

5m beading thread
178 1.6-mm cylinder beads (blue-green)
434 1.6-mm cylinder beads (cream)
40 1.6-mm cylinder beads (pale blue)
32 1.6-mm cylinder beads (blue)
29 1.5-mm (15/0) seed beads (cream)
4-mm round crystal bead (milky white)
4 x 10-mm tube bead
Strap finding

1 Weave strap in odd-count peyote stitch.

❶ Cut a 1.5-m length of thread. String a stopper bead, leaving a 20-cm end. Add a blue-green bead, 7 cream cylinder beads and another blue-green bead (Fig. 1).

❷ Weave Row 3, referring to drawing for color placement (Fig. 2).

❸ Turn to prepare for Row 4: Pass needle back 2 rows and 3 stitches, changing direction as shown in drawing. Pass through bead at left edge of Row 3 again, and begin Row 4 (Fig. 3).

❹ Weave Rows 5 and 6, referring to drawing. Turn to prepare for Row 6. Pass needle back 3 rows and 2 stitches, then turn, passing through bead at left edge of Row 5. Begin Row 6 (Fig. 4).

❺ Continue weaving, referring to drawing for color placement, until you have 152 rows. Be sure to make turns on the edge with the stopper bead, as directed in Step ④ to prepare for next row (Fig. 5).

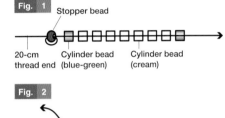

Fig. 1
Stopper bead
20-cm thread end
Cylinder bead (blue-green)
Cylinder bead (cream)

Fig. 2
←Row 3

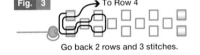

Fig. 3
To Row 4
Go back 2 rows and 3 stitches.

Fig. 4
Row 4→
←Row 5
Go back 3 rows and 2 stitches

TIPS

■ Turn at starting edge to change direction of thread.

When you work even-count peyote stitch, you always pass through a bead from the previous row and then begin the next row. But with odd-count peyote stitch, you end by stringing a bead, so there is nowhere to go (see Fig. 2). To surmount this problem, we need to change the direction of the thread, in other words, turn. Usually you go down 2 rows and 3 stitches to prepare for the 4th row, and down 3 rows and 2 stitches thereafter.

■ You can tell the difference between odd-count and even-count stitches.

Flat pieces woven in odd-count peyote stitch look a little different than even-count stitches. In even-count peyote, the beginning of the first row (the first stitch) is recessed, while the last stitch protrudes. In odd-count peyote, both the first and last stitches protrude. Once you learn to recognize the difference, you'll spot these two types of stitches without having to count.

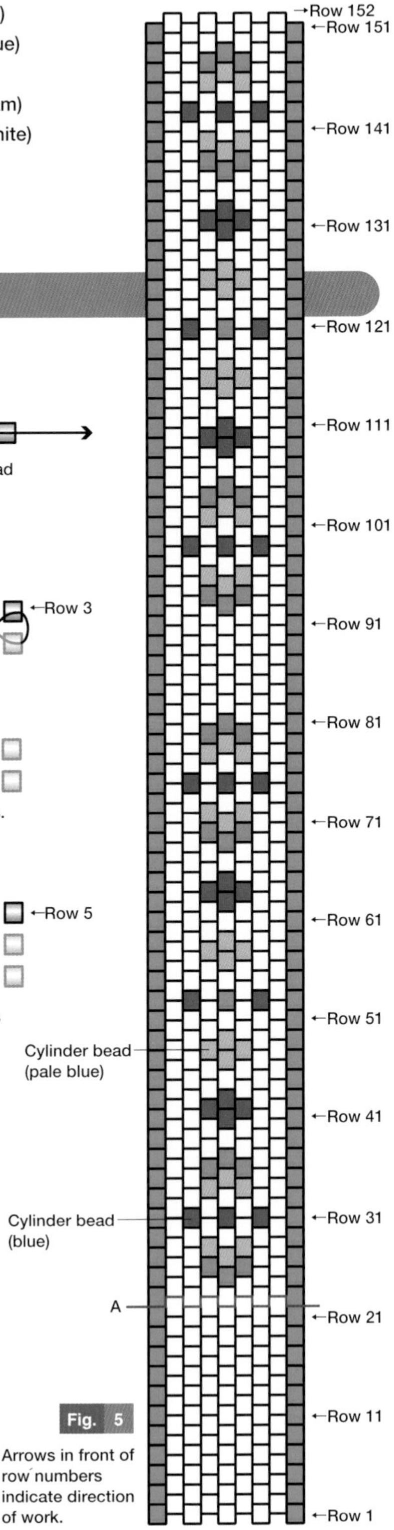

→Row 152
←Row 151
←Row 141
←Row 131
←Row 121
←Row 111
←Row 101
←Row 91
←Row 81
←Row 71
←Row 61
←Row 51
Cylinder bead (pale blue)
←Row 41
Cylinder bead (blue)
←Row 31
A
←Row 21
Fig. 5
←Row 11
←Row 1

※Arrows in front of row numbers indicate direction of work.

2 | Join edges of strap and attach to strap finding.

❶ You will be joining each end of strap to A
(Fig. 6).

❷ With thread at end of work, join the row under A
(Row 21) to last row (Row 152), passing through
beads from each end in alternation. Pass needle
through beads near end of work and finish off
thread (Fig. 7).

❸ Remove stopper bead at beginning of work.
Using that thread, join the row under A to Row 1,
passing through beads in alternation. Finish off
thread (Fig. 8).

❹ Attach strap finding. Insert tube bead* into small
loop at beginning of work (Fig. 9).

❺ Cut a 50-cm length of thread. Leaving a 10-cm
end, pass needle through tube bead. Add 1.5-
mm seed beads, a crystal bead and strap
finding, to form a loop, referring to drawing
(Fig. 10).

❻ Pass needle back through beads in loop twice
more. Tie thread to thread at beginning of work
in a square knot. Finish off both threads by
passing through 2-3 adjacent beads; cut excess
at edge of a bead.

※ If you don't have a tube bead, substitute several
beads that will fit snugly into the loop.

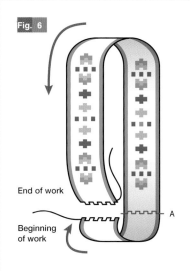

Fig. 6

End of work

Beginning
of work

A

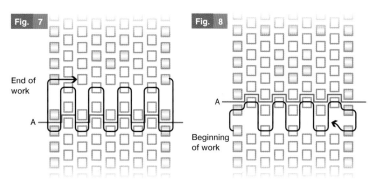

Fig. 7

End of
work

A

Fig. 8

A

Beginning
of work

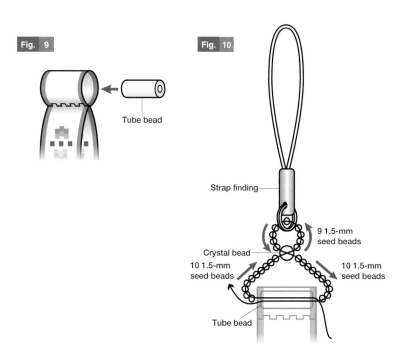

Fig. 9

Tube bead

Fig. 10

Strap finding

9 1.5-mm
seed beads

Crystal bead

10 1.5-mm
seed beads

10 1.5-mm
seed beads

Tube bead

Badge Brooch

■Finished measurements:

3cm W x 7cm L (Peyote stitch: 3.5cm)

■Supplies

3.5m beading thread
131 1.6-mm cylinder beads (silver)

169 1.6-mm cylinder beads (metallic blue)
21 1.6-mm cylinder beads (bronze)
166 1.5-mm (15/0) seed beads (silver)
36 1.5-mm (15/0) seed beads (blue)
3-mm round fire-polished bead (CAL)
4 3-mm round fire-polished beads (sky blue)
4-mm round fire-polished bead (CAL)
3 4-mm round fire-polished beads (sky blue)
5-mm round fire-polished bead (sky blue)
6-mm round fire-polished bead (pale blue)
4 3-mm bicone crystal beads (translucent)
3 4-mm bicone crystal beads (translucent)
5-mm bicone crystal bead (translucent)
Brooch back (silver)

1 Weave brooch in odd-count peyote stitch.

❶ Cut a 2-m length of thread. String a stopper bead, leaving a 30-cm end. Weave 3 19-stitch rows of peyote stitch with silver cylinder beads (Fig. 1).

❷ Turn to prepare for Row 4: Pass needle back 2 rows and 3 stitches, changing direction as shown in drawing. Pass through bead at left edge of Row 3 again (Fig. 2).

❸ Weave Rows 4-29, referring to drawing (no increases or decreases). On the edge with stopper bead, be sure to go back 3 rows and 2 stitches and turn (see p. 40) to prepare for next row (Fig. 3).

❹ Starting in Rows 30, decrease one stitch at each edge. Pass needle back 3 rows and 3 stitches and turn, as described in Step ②, to make one decrease. Make decreases in Rows 30 and 31 following this procedure (Figs. 3, 4 and 5).

TIP

■ When decreasing, make same turns as you do at one edge of odd-count peyote stitch.

When you decrease, you go back 3 rows and 3 stitches and turn, just as you do at one edge of odd-count peyote stitch. When you decrease, the thread path of the beads at the edges should be diagonal. It's possible to make decreases on just one side of a woven piece. But with odd-count peyote stitch, your piece will look nicer if you decrease one stitch at each edge, with one stitch remaining right in the center.

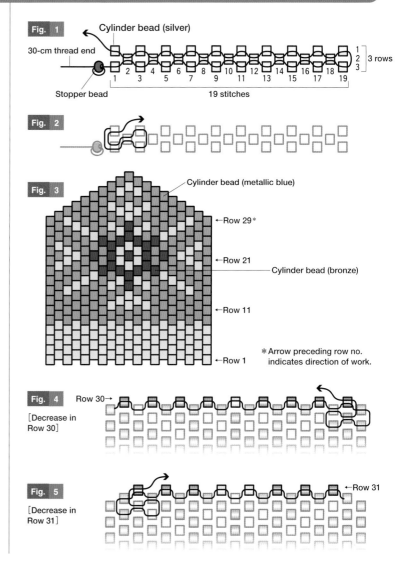

❺ From Row 32 on, you will be decreasing at each edge, making turns as described in previous step. At Row 38, you should have one stitch left (Fig. 6).

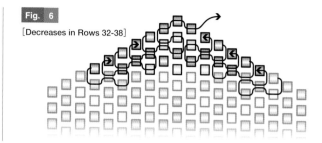

Fig. 6

[Decreases in Rows 32-38]

2 Attach fringe and complete brooch.

❶ Attach fringe to bottom of brooch: with thread at end of Row 37, pass through beads in brooch, referring to drawing. Bring needle out at Row 38. Make fringe in the order indicated in drawings. Each set of fringe will consist of 2 strands. Attach one set, then pass through 6-mm fire-polished bead and 1.5-mm seed beads and pass needle back into beads in brooch. Make next set of fringe. Repeat until you have made 4 sets of fringe, or 8 strands. Pass needle through beads in brooch and finish off thread (Figs. 7 and 8).

❷ Join Rows 1 and 8 to make a hem. Remove stopper bead, thread needle and go down 3 rows and over 2 stitches. pass through beads in Rows 1 and 8 in alternation to join. Run needle through beads and finish off thread (Figs. 9 & 10).

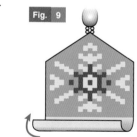

Fig. 9

❸ Decorate perimeter of brooch: cut a 1-mm length of thread. String a stopper bead, leaving a 20-cm end. Add silver 1.5-mm seed beads, passing through beads at edge of brooch as you go along, and referring to drawing. Finish off threads at beginning and end of work (Fig. 11).

❹ Attach brooch back to wrong side of brooch: cut a 50-cm length of thread. Sew brooch back to brooch, passing through beads as you go along. Run needle back through beads and finish off thread (Fig. 12).

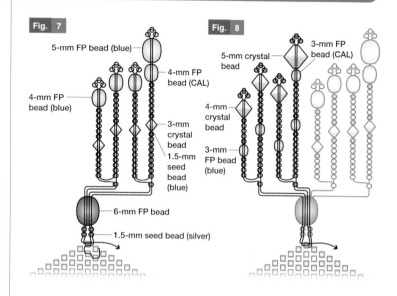

Fig. 7

5-mm FP bead (blue)

4-mm FP bead (CAL)

4-mm FP bead (blue)

3-mm crystal bead

1.5-mm seed bead (blue)

6-mm FP bead

1.5-mm seed bead (silver)

Fig. 8

5-mm crystal bead

3-mm FP bead (CAL)

4-mm crystal bead

3-mm FP bead (blue)

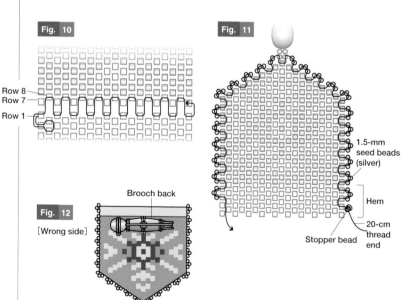

Fig. 10

Row 8
Row 7

Row 1

Fig. 11

1.5-mm seed beads (silver)

Hem

20-cm thread end

Stopper bead

Fig. 12

[Wrong side]

Brooch back

Flower Garden Choker

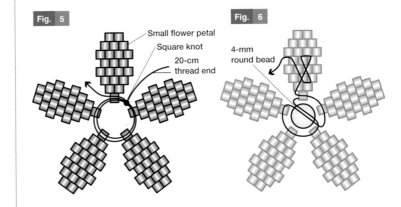

■Finished measurements:

2.5-4.5cm W x 42.5cm L
(Flower diameter: 2.5cm (small), 3cm (large))

■Supplies

19.2m beading thread
385 1.6-mm cylinder beads (black)
818 1.6-mm cylinder beads (matte black)
634 2-mm (11/0) seed beads (black)
32 3-mm drop beads (black)
4 4-mm round beads (translucent)
5-mm round bead (translucent)
Hook-and-eye clasp
2 5-mm split rings (gunmetal)

1 Make petals and make flower motifs.

❶ Make petals for small flower motifs: cut a 50-cm length of thread. String a stopper bead, leaving a 20-cm thread end. Add 8 black cylinder beads. You have completed Rows 1 and 2.

❷ Complete Row 3, then pass through first bead strung (Bead 1), moving downward, toward Row 1 (Fig. 1).

❸ In Row 4, you will be weaving below starting point, passing through beads in Row 1. Pass through Bead 8 and bring needle out at right edge of piece (Fig. 2).

❹ Pass through Bead 9 in Row 5 and move upward, passing through beads in Row 3 as you weave. Pass through first bead strung (Bead 1) (Fig. 2).

❺ Row 6: pass through Beads 2 and 13, then move downward, passing through beads in Row 4. Continue in the same way, passing through beads at edges, until you have woven 7 rows. Pass through Bead 1. Finish off threads at beginning and end of work, passing through beads in woven piece. Make 10 petals with black cylinder beads and 10 more with matte black cylinder beads (Fig. 3).

❻ Make 5 petals for large flower motif in the same way, using black cylinder beads. String 10 beads for first 2 rows, then weave 9 rows, referring to drawing (Fig. 4).

❼ Assemble flower motifs: cut a 50-cm length of thread, and pass through Bead 1 on 5 of the small flower petals. Pass thread through beads again, moving in same direction. Tie threads in a square knot, leaving 20-cm ends. Pass through first bead again (Fig. 5).

❽ Add 4-mm round bead and pass through beads on petals, referring to drawing. Pass needle through beads in petals and finish off thread. Assemble other motifs in same way (Fig. 6).

❾ Assemble large flower motif in same way, adding a 5-mm round bead at center.

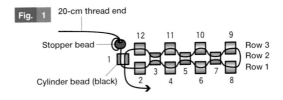

Fig. 1

20-cm thread end
Stopper bead
Cylinder bead (black)
Row 3 Row 2 Row 1

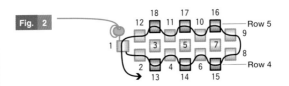

Fig. 2

Row 5 Row 4

Fig. 3 Make 20 small petals (10 black/ 10 matte black).

Row 7 Row 6

Fig. 4 Make 5 petals for large motif (black).

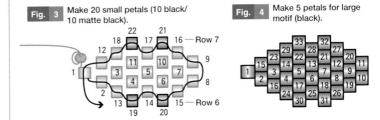

Fig. 5

Small flower petal
Square knot
20-cm thread end

Fig. 6

4-mm round bead

2 Join flower motifs and complete choker.

❶ You will be placing large flower motif at center, and joining 2 small motifs (one black and one matte black) at each side of large motif, referring to drawing. Note that a-1 and a-2, which go between motifs, are woven in the same way, but in left-right mirror image. The same applies to b-1 and b-2, which go between motif and closure (Fig. 7).

❷ Join large motif and small motif A (a-1 in Fig. 7): cut an 80-cm length of thread. Run needle through beads in A to finish off one end of thread. String 2-mm seed beads, a drop bead and cylinder beads, referring to drawing. Finish off thread as you did other end at starting point. Following same procedure, join Motifs A and B (a-1 in Fig. 7), large motif and Motif C (a-2 in Fig. 7), and Motifs C and D (a-2 in Fig. 7) (Figs. 8 & 9).

❸ Attach closure to Motif B (b-1 in Fig. 7): cut an 80-cm length of thread, run needle through beads in motif to finish off one end of thread. String 2-mm seed beads, a drop bead and cylinder beads on thread, referring to drawing. Insert split ring into hook of closure, and join to choker with 2-mm seed beads. Pass thread through beads in loop again (Fig. 10).

❹ Weave back toward Motif B and add new beads to motif, referring to drawing. Pass needle through beads in Motif B and finish off thread (Fig. 11).

❺ Attach eye of closure to Motif D (b-2 in Fig. 7) in the same way. Finish off thread.

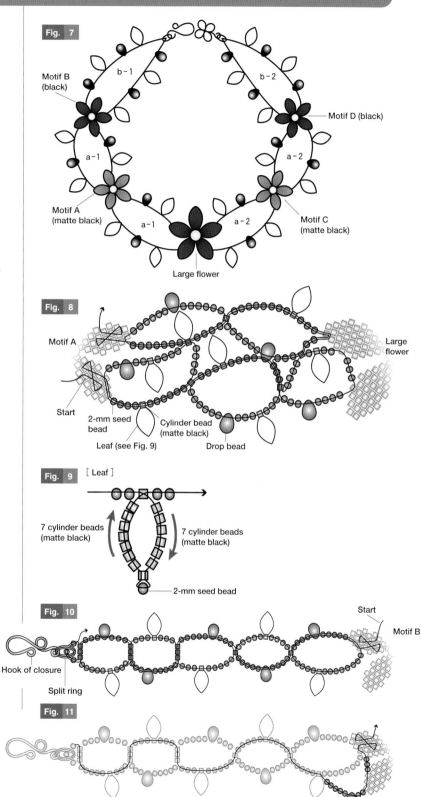

Fig. 7

Motif B (black)
b-1
b-2
Motif D (black)
a-1
a-2
Motif A (matte black)
a-1
a-2
Motif C (matte black)
Large flower

Fig. 8

Motif A
Large flower
Start
2-mm seed bead
Cylinder bead (matte black)
Leaf (see Fig. 9)
Drop bead

Fig. 9 [Leaf]

7 cylinder beads (matte black)
7 cylinder beads (matte black)
2-mm seed bead

Fig. 10

Hook of closure
Split ring
Start
Motif B

Fig. 11

About the author: Kumiko Mizuno Ito

Beadwork artist and consultant Kumiko Mizuno Ito is a graduate of Sophia University. A former knitting instructor, she currently specializes in beading techniques. She discovered bead stitching in the U.S., and since then has been instrumental in popularizing the art in Japan. In addition to designing and creating jewelry and other beadwork, Ms. Mizuno organizes workshops, prepares curricula for certified beadwork classes, and writes instructional beading books. Among her publications as author/editor are Beadweaving with Needle and Thread (Maria Shobo), Beading Color Schemes Made Easy, Strategies for Perfecting Your Beading Skills and Easy Beading Stitches (all issued by Patchwork Tsushin).

BEADWEAVING BRILLIANCE
MAKE BEAUTIFUL JEWELRY AS YOU LEARN OFF-LOOM TECHNIQUES

By Kumiko Mizuno Ito
Even beginners can create exquisite accessories with this detailed, step-by-step guide to mastering off-loom beading techniques. Just in time for holiday hand-made-gift giving comes this beautifully illustrated book that shows crafters how to create colorful and unique beaded accessories. Using a single needle and thread, readers will learn a variety of stitches, including herringbone, peyote (also known as gourd), brick, square, right angle weave and African helix, to weave beads into a flat fabric or 3-dimensional object.

82 pp. 8 1/4 × 10 1/8 in., full-color throughout.
ISBN : 978-4-88996-225-3

US $ 18.00